The Ten Books of "I'LL TEACH YOU MY JOB!"

By Ken Tagawa

Five sentences...

- I hire people who can do my job.

- I want to make you so good that others will want to hire you.

- While it would be great if you stayed with us, I expect you to leave within a couple of years or perhaps three to five.

- My job is to get you ready!

And Watch It Happen Every Day!

- **And to get you ready, I will teach you my job!**

These words certainly are not what any of us have learned to say, been told to say, or expect to hear.

But whether you're a manager – just starting out or experienced, a supervisor, a division head, a team leader, an executive — the CEO or president, or an employee…

take a minute and roll these words around in your mind.

If you said them to yourself, would you think differently? Do they make you think of doing something in your job differently?

And if you said these words to those who worked with and for you,

"I'll Teach You My Job!"

what impact do you think these words would have on them?

I know those words had impact…

because when I said those words to people who worked with and for me or to those who were candidates for jobs,

they all kind of smiled and looked at me with an expression of…

"Did I just hear what I think I just heard?"

If we're the individuals who are "in charge" with people reporting to you as part of a group, team, office, or work unit,

And Watch It Happen Every Day!

teaching your job will change the dynamics of the workplace...

driving amazing changes in effectiveness and productivity that everyone would like to achieve!

"I'll Teach You My Job!"

Table of Contents

For you, the reader of this book, this is how you read this book.   11

Books 1 through 4
"Struggling and Then... Magically Coming to Grips with Managing!"

Book 1 — "I Never Expected... Struggling, Magic, and BAM! Sudden Lightning Bolts!   16

Book 2 — What a Manager Has to Do... Subtraction and Get Rid of the Egregiously Bad   35

Book 3 — Connecting More Than Just Dots   75

Book 4.1 — Realizing What It Takes   102

Book 4.2 — Coming Together on Managing   126

Books 5 through 8
"If You've Not Gotten the Results You Expected..."

And Watch It Happen Every Day!

Book 5 — "Adults!" The Breakthrough to
Managing Well!   147

Book 6 — "You Can't Change People. You Can Only
Change the Way You Work with Them"   187

Book 7 — The Book Specifically for Those of Us
"Who Are in Charge"   216

Book 8 — The Twice-Weekly Meetings… Some
Hold Them Every Day or Twice-a-Day   257

Books 9 and 10
"Revisiting Our Jobs So That We Ensure Astounding Success"

Book 9 — "Teaching My Job… A Revisit to
Struggling, Magic, and BAM! Even More Lightning
Bolts~   313

Book 9.1 — Teaching My Job… Managing Themes
and a Set of Current Plus Two New Activities   316

Book 9.2 — Teaching My Job... To Manage Well, Add Two More — the Third and Fourth — Activities Not Usually Discussed   374

Book 10 – Are We Done Yet? No, We're Just Beginning... The Concrete Deliverables for Building Extraordinary Organizational Capacity   438

The Appendix: How to Read this Book   464

And Watch It Happen Every Day!

Like Flipping a Switch!

I didn't write this book to say once more what thousands of others have already written and gotten wrong. Written as a fascinating personal narrative that any manager, supervisor, employee, team leader, division head, or executive can identify with.

And in telling this compelling story of how a manager... struggling to do his job and work with those in his group... **BAM!**

HAD THAT BIG, GLARING LIGHT BULB GO ON — SOMETIMES IT FELT MORE LIKE A HUGE LIGHTNING BOLT!

and by making some simple changes which all of us can do, and, most importantly, do as part of the work we do every day, created a remarkable place of heart, connection, commitment, and astounding results!

Want to Have that Place Where We'd All Want to Work?

"TEACH YOUR JOB"

and Watch It Happen Every Day!

"I'll Teach You My Job!"

Available in three other formats:

A 3-volume 6x9 softcover bookset.
Excellent for a home library or reading table.

A convenient 7-volume softcover bookset.
As the volumes are in an easy-to-carry, slimmer 5x8 format that slips into a personal bag/coat pocket, each volume can be readily shared with your team/group.

As an e-book.

And Watch It Happen Every Day!

_____

©2020 Kenneth M. Tagawa

All rights reserved. No part of this publication may be reproduced, distributed, or transmitted in any form or by any means, including photocopying, recording, or other electronic or mechanical methods, without the prior written permission of the author, except for quotation of material to be included in book reviews and other noncommercial use as permitted by copyright law. For permission requests, write the author,

kentagawa@NYauthor@gmail.com

ISBN: 9798667883227

"I'll Teach You My Job!"

For you, the reader of this book...

This is a book to be used — *this is your book so **make it your own!** One of the first things you can do* — ***write in it!** Write your name/contact info on the cover or the back of the front cover.*

*Also **write on the title page**,*

> *"If you find this book, please return to me as this is an important book with information that really is meaningful to me!"*

Again, print your name, phone number, and write down the date!

Second: *To get the most out of this book, there are pages for notes at the end of this book. You are encouraged to use those pages to write your reactions, a thought to do something, or a reminder to share with your colleagues/group.*

You can use color pens or markers or pencils to circle, underline, or highlight any info so that that info stands out! Draw arrows linking two things or cross-reference page numbers.

And Watch It Happen Every Day!
_____

Third: These thoughts/ideas to test, try out and share and perhaps develop into a new program or service — a new way of how things get done... **are your "takeaways."**

While authors in many books summarize the takeaways for you at the end of a chapter, as I don't know your group or what you're responsible for, what I think really **isn't as important as what you come up with on your own!** Your own takeaways are certainly going to be much more useful for you!

Also date whatever you write down. You'll be surprised at how the date — even where you were — when you thought of something will be a strong prompt that will powerfully remind you, perhaps even recommit you, so that your thought leads to something useful.

As you read this book, you'll notice its layout is just different.

This book is written in a **special "easy-to-read and quick to learn" layout**. You'll see larger fonts, bolding of words and sentences for emphasis, unique line spacing...

"I'll Teach You My Job!"

*and changes in grammar and phrasing that would **cause your English teacher to just yell!***

"No! No! NO!!! That's totally unacceptable! You can't do that!!

I call this the "Tagawa Mastery Format" and you can read the Appendix — "How To Read This Book" — at the end of this book and get an explanation how I came to write the book in this style/layout.

And Watch It Happen Every Day!
_____

Want to know more about Ken Tagawa?

See his LinkedIn Profile.

Books 1 through 4

"Struggling and Then... Magically Coming to Grips with Managing!"

Book 1 — "I Never Expected... Struggling, Magic, and BAM! Sudden Lightning Bolts!

Book 2 — What a Manager Has to Do... Subtraction and Get Rid of the Egregiously Bad

Book 3 — Connecting More Than Just Dots

Book 4.1 — Realizing What It Takes

Book 4.2 — Coming Together on Managing

And Watch It Happen Every Day!

Book 1 — "I Never Expected... Struggling, Magic, and BAM! Sudden Lightning Bolts!"

So, one day, I sat back, and it just hit me…

Was I managing and leading? Hardly, I was struggling. I felt like I was pushing a wet noodle.

Can you manage and lead if you really don't know much about what's going on — what people are working on?

Of course not, but there I was, trying to manage and lead when **I didn't have a decent grasp** as to what everyone was doing…

"I'll Teach You My Job!"

I felt frustrated and stupid at the same time, but I also knew **I needed to somehow get that grip...**

That my early managerial jobs were challenging is something that each of us has experienced.

But even after I had held more jobs, I still found there were problems and issues that just "popped up" and had to be taken care of.

This first book describes critical realizations and actions — which in retrospect were obvious...

to take that put me on the journey to managerial effectiveness.

And by enabling me to work effectively with people,

I become not just a better manager, but an individual who could say, **I now knew what it takes to manage well!**

And Watch It Happen Every Day!

So, the first thing I tried was the standing meeting every day.

We had been meeting once every two weeks and to now meet EVERY DAY was an abrupt change and... **people couldn't believe they had to stand while we met!**

But we weren't meeting just to be meeting. **In every meeting I started asking** what people were working on...

And out of that, over the days and weeks, came a huge list of what each person was doing, had to do,

but also a surprising number of things that I knew nothing about... **but nonetheless had to be taken care of.**

"I'll Teach You My Job!"

So, our meetings became not just, "What are you doing today and tomorrow and the rest of this week?"...

They become "What do you have to do this month and next month and the month after that"...

until finally we had a whole year — the full cycle of things we had to do, of deadlines... of preparation and organizational activities.

So, we knew much better which materials to develop, the events and meetings to schedule, and also the mailings to send out.

And as we all knew the tasks to make this all happen... **not only did we now know** who would be taking on the tasks that had to be done,

And Watch It Happen Every Day!

we also knew the follow-up that would assure that we were doing everything we needed to do.

Of course, while **this was exhausting for everyone,** it was also exhilarating!

You could see the spark ignite!

They were hearing for the first time what each other was doing!

But they did dread coming to the next day's meeting because they knew **they'd be asked** if they had done what they said they had to do the previous day.

With unexpected interruptions and crises —

phone calls, urgent drop-ins from employees and managers, having to be out of the office for a doctor's appointment,

a meeting at your kids' schools or other personal/family concerns...

or being at meetings that lasted longer than scheduled and so on,

no one was always getting everything done...

They did revolt a bit, so we went to meeting twice a week — Tuesday and Thursday morning first thing and instead of standing...

I relented and we also all did sit — around a four-sided square meeting table.

And Watch It Happen Every Day!

Then something magical started to happen...

Somebody would talk about something they didn't get done or were working on...

something that was going on and had been brought to their attention, or a problem they had encountered.

And someone else would say,

"Oh, I know something about that," or, "That same person came to see me," or, "I had that same thing come up."

And Jerelle and Sharice would connect... **and piece together** the puzzle and come up with a better approach and solution.

Eventually it became obvious that those not at the meeting — the receptionist, the records clerk, a technical staff member also knew something.

But we didn't know they did until their managers went back to give them a debrief about the meeting they had been in with me...

and those who had not been in the meeting would say they knew something about that problem or issue.

They said enough things with enough of a different slant **that showed us that we** were working with incomplete information — that we didn't fully know what was going on.

So "Click!" — the light went on...

And Watch It Happen Every Day!
_____

and I threw out the organizational chart —

Yes, whether it's the office or group I was in charge of or it's your team or unit or your leadership group, can any of us really say, who reports to whom and the layers we have is the best way to get things done?

While beyond the scope of this book, we've all assumed that the way we're structured is the "best way."

But given the number of times things don't quite come together or some important work doesn't get done,

it's not unreasonable to question whether we're really organized the "best way."

At the time, because my career had been as the lead troubleshooter in our organization... I had been asked to take over and fix an HR operation.

So, the changes I made caused considerable panic....

"I'll Teach You My Job!"

and nearly caused a revolution among the managers in the office.

The benefits tech wasn't going to report to the benefits manager?

The compensation specialist wasn't going to report the employment manager?

The receptionist wasn't going to report to the office's administrative assistant

And so on…

No one, I repeat, **no one had ever done that**… and just who were they going to report to?

Me!...

And Watch It Happen Every Day!

Me, because **I realized that I wasn't getting** the full picture.

Communication wasn't flowing — important information was getting lost in translation from one person to another or not surfacing at all.

And I knew that **without that full picture,** I as well as everyone working in our group would not fully know what was going on... and who was doing what.

And because we didn't know, we would continue to make mistakes... and there would be continued delays in getting things done.

So, **not by any grand design,** but because everyone ended up reporting to me, we became a flat organization — at the time when no one knew what a flat organization was!

And unexpectedly **the dynamics of the office** changed amazingly…

Managers who at first didn't like losing the people who reported to them… **suddenly found that they liked** not having that responsibility for supervising someone else's work.

However, they didn't like not being able to dump (I mean assign…) a difficult or boring matter onto someone else because that problem was now theirs and theirs alone.

Well, it **wasn't quite true** that it was theirs alone.

What happened again, magically but on a greater scale, was that when they talked about the problem, others — including those who previously reported to the manager

And Watch It Happen Every Day!

and who oftentimes wouldn't speak up out of deference or to avoid coming across as challenging their manager's view —

began speaking up and sharing what they knew and then pitched in to solve the problem.

And we really started to evolve more complete/whole pictures of the problems and then craft really fitting solutions!

And **the managers changed** also — that is, those who had been managers (they were no longer managers of people but managers of programs)...

learned not to direct, but to ask for help... asking if others knew about this problem or situation,

and that simple act of asking for help **changed the climate** of the office and —again, nearly magically —

it felt like it happened overnight...

our work relationships **changed from hierarchical and directive... to collegial, collaborative, and communicative!**

All good for sure!

We're making a lot of positive progress... getting on top of things — the daily operational stuff and I knew much better what was going on,

but just because we had had a little success, we **couldn't get complacent...**

There was much more... And what was that "much more?"

And Watch It Happen Every Day!
_____

Ask any manager, any supervisor or executive,

ask any employee…

and they'll tell you about the stuff that makes coming to work not such a great experience… stuff that makes their stomachs churn and their heads hurt…

They will tell you about stuff that you and they carry home every night it seems…

that keeps you and them awake and

perhaps a bit hesitant about coming to work the next day,

or perhaps even causing you/them to want to look for another job.

"I'll Teach You My Job!"

And even though everyone knows about these issues/challenges, they're tough and nobody is really ready to take them on...

to do something to take care of these issues, problems, or situations.

So, even though we were better and as much as I/we felt were had made amazing progress and liked getting on top of what we were doing...

certain things beyond the operational **wouldn't go away.**

These situations/challenges happened in my group... and through conversations with numerous others who were also managers or supervisors or executives,

it was clear that everyone was facing these challenges as well.

And Watch It Happen Every Day!
_____

And what were these challenges?

These are the knotty things that go on between/among people in offices — sometimes work-related but which were also interpersonal interactions...

and on some occasions with those to whom they report — which means us!

We kept hearing about them — but I was so busy and we were so busy as a group trying to fix the operational...

that we didn't have time to think about them, much less do something to fix them.

But they don't go away... they just **don't go away.**

"I'll Teach You My Job!"

___

And as these problems kept popping up, they reminded us that we had other business — important business to take care of that required my attention.

So, as much as I'd like to tie up this first book by going back and sharing what we had accomplished and that we felt good about what we had done —

>by pointing out that we had come up with **a unique way to work together...**

>that by getting in sync — leading us to unexpectedly and surprisingly turn things around so that we felt that we were not only doing good things but were really **moving in the right direction...**

And Watch It Happen Every Day!

as much sense as it made to think that we should build on what we had done and move on/focus on our next positive steps,

I knew that so long as these difficult, long-neglected situations involving egregiously bad people were allowed to exist in our groups, teams, and offices,

we clearly had challenges that now had to be taken care of.

Book 2 — What a Manager Has to Do… Subtraction and Get Rid of the Egregiously Bad

Subtraction? Really?

As a manager or executive — and for sure as an employee, we absolutely know these egregious, gut-wrenching problems exist and **continue to** plague us!

And what's even worse, as we also know no one is doing much about them… that it's rare that anything is done about these folks,

and as you may also feel that you **can't do much** either, it shouldn't come as a surprise that these individuals with their bad attitudes and bad behaviors…

And Watch It Happen Every Day!

are just problems that **we have resigned ourselves** to putting up with.

When I had begun my career, I was fortunate to work with a vice-president who, as a former bomber pilot who had made bombing runs through flak-filled skies, was tough as nails, had nerves of steel, and was really demanding.

He told me something/ made me do two things that has always served me well.

Read and know every policy, administrative procedure, and strategic document and then also know the detail of every account. In this second book, you'll see that knowing policy is how to take on and resolve challenges that have stymied/frustrated many who "are in charge."

"I'll Teach You My Job!"

So, what that leads us to think, even though these people — not just employees but also administrators and executives — make my stomach churn,

is that, as I don't also need to make the situation worse by taking on these people…

and as long as **whatever is going on** is tolerable and I can put up with it,

I don't need the headache that would undoubtedly happen if I took them on.

While some of us might **think it's reasonable** to handle these situations this way because doing so gets us through the day,

the problem is… what if it isn't tolerable? What if one of these people says or does something that is completely unacceptable?

And Watch It Happen Every Day!

In the back of your mind, you know — as things aren't getting better and are likely getting worse,

that day is coming where you will have to do something.

Because the consequence is that, if you don't do anything, without any question, your inaction **will undermine you and keep you trapped** in an intolerable situation.

For me, I was somewhat surprised when I came up against these kinds of people and problems.

But knowing that I wanted to do a good job and to be highly effective... and **I also believe that most of us** also want to do a great job at work...

the thought of having to put up with these people was simply unacceptable to me.

Thus, I found myself spending many hours trying to

figure out how to deal with them. And one day, again, I had that **BAM experience!**

And it came to me... what I had to do.

"What simply came into my mind was a single word,

"SUBTRACTION"

SUBTRACTION? Why subtraction...

Because this word — which most of us never think of using,

told me/tells you **how to break out** and end the feeling that I was/you were "locked into" these unacceptable people.

And Watch It Happen Every Day!

And once you realize that **you also can get rid of** those who were causing these intolerable situations,

just like I experienced things turning around, I believe that you also will not only become much more effective...

you may even find yourself waking up and actually **looking forward** to coming to work!

So, "Subtraction" leads you to act!

Repeat: You can act — whether you're a manager, a supervisor, or an executive.

I know you can... because I did it... I did it when I was a manager without a lot of experience and had to deal with these egregiously bad people and difficult situations!

"I'll Teach You My Job!"

(And what and how I and those who worked with and for me were able to do this will be discussed later in this book.)

Will taking action be worth it?

Absolutely!

Because... once you've taken care of these problems... by getting rid of these people or **putting them in their place —**

your office, team, or workgroup will also stop having those gut-wrenching knots in their stomachs... and, best of all...

And Watch It Happen Every Day!

because they know that what's unacceptable was handled by you…

you will be also be seen as amazingly more effective!

So, let's turn to examples of these egregiously bad people/situations — what we've called for years, **"the big dead moose."**

And whether you have some of them or all of them or even more, we're going to deal with them and "kick those dead moose off the table!"

Where to start:

While we were a diverse office, others were not… and

"I'll Teach You My Job!"

---

supervisors and managers had **paralyzing racial climate** issues.

In other units, supervisors were **being abusive, yelling** at employees,

and we had a bunch of allegations about discrimination and harassment.

There were also incidents of **workplace violence...**

But that's not all...

People were told to work overtime — being told to come in for evening or weekend events beyond the workday when they didn't want to... and they weren't being paid.

And Watch It Happen Every Day!
_____

Then we **had instances** where people were getting overtime pay who shouldn't have... because their boss thought they were underpaid but couldn't get them promoted.

While this may not seem important... none of us really knew how to bring a new person on board.

We just assumed that people come to work to do a job... which is the way most of us think about work.

That is, working was a job for which you got hired to do certain things and few of us when we come on board have any sense that there might be something more.

But if we **want a better group** as well as to be part of a business/organization to work in and for... a place where people would want to work...

"I'll Teach You My Job!"

---

we had to raise the bar.

We had to convey somehow what we as a group and this organization stood for — so that people could understand... why, beyond a paycheck, should they want to work here?

As I said in Book 1, because we weren't on top of what we were doing — because we were making too many mistakes and spending so much time fixing what we had messed up,

we were so consumed with trying to get the day-to-day stuff done that... we didn't have time or energy left to deal with these problems.

However, once we began to get our operational house in order, **we were freeing** up our time, and could

And Watch It Happen Every Day!

begin to think about taking on and dealing with these pervasive long-neglected problems.

So, with the backdrop of knowing about all of these challenges, it would have been easy for me — as the person "in charge" —

to put together a plan — a "strategic plan" —

> something you can also do or may have already had experience doing...

with a set of operational priorities focused on these problems.

But being effective is not about planning. It's about **doing something** and doing the right something!

So, because it was critical to get this right, rather than

doing what a manager would normally do — crafting that plan and putting it out there to solicit input and feedback,

I got struck by a lightning bolt!

We had had success in the operational stuff...

because we got on top of what we had to do by involving everyone so that we could understand what we were doing and therefore how best to get organized.

Could we do something similarly to take on these long-standing challenges?

And Watch It Happen Every Day!
___

And as **I began to raise** these egregious problems, and just as I had come to know that everyone knew the problems in our operational work,

it was no surprise that they — like Fiona and Damon — also knew about and had experience with these challenges.

Yet even though we had had amazing success where magically everything came together to solve our operational problems and…

while it was reasonable therefore to assume that we could also take on these problems, somehow these **challenges were going to be different.**

Taking on these long-standing problems —

    these terrible egregious problems —

"I'll Teach You My Job!"

the huge dead moose that everyone saw but no one had done anything about for years…

was not the same as fixing operational problems and figuring out processes.

These were **simply different, something more…**

And as we talked, what we came to realize is that **these problems were about** the nature of who we were and our organization,

and that taking on these problems meant we were going to have to face one of the biggest challenges in any business or organization — which was to **change the culture.**

And Watch It Happen Every Day!

And, as the key to changing the culture was having everyone know what the organization stood for...

we knew we had to send a message that those who were the badly egregious would know that **they'd have to change or move on.**

GETTING STARTED:

Just as we had gone through the "what did we have to do today, tomorrow, this week, month and year"... to get our operational responsibilities in order,

We sought to **get that grasp** for taking on these organizational issues...

and embarked on a strategic planning retreat so that we would understand, get organized and do what was needed to take on these problems.

"I'll Teach You My Job!"

We did the usual approach to a strategic plan which is to do an environment scan —

a huge brainstorm and put everything up — over a hundred items...

on the board for all of us to see what could possibly be of concern to us or impact us or the people working in the organization.

As we did this exercise... it was not surprising to see that these long-standing **"dead moose" problems kept popping** up in various forms and situations.

But while the magnitude of the issues was a bit unnerving... how could things have gotten this bad?

it was good that we could begin to see clearly what we faced.

And Watch It Happen Every Day!

What followed then was a SWOT analysis — **S**trengths, **W**eaknesses, **O**pportunities, and **T**hreats regarding these composite groupings...

where, in having nailed down as clearly as possible what we would need to take on,

we had to ask whether we had the capacity — the strength we could turn to and utilize to resolve these issues.

>(I soon came to realize this concern was unwarranted which I'll explain later.)

I led the whole retreat for two days and, of course, it was exhausting for me and... frankly, the interest on the part of others waned noticeably and understandably at times.

"I'll Teach You My Job!"

But, as we came to understand these problems, as we began to see the outline of **what our future might be...**

a better-run organization — one where the wrong stuff that was going on would be minimized or stopped,

> an organization where people would begin to see and begin to believe that things were getting better,
>
> a place where people would begin to look forward to coming to work every day,
>
> a place where the organizational climate was not going to stay what it had been for years but had begun to shift...

our optimism grew and we came away with a sense that we did have a shot at changing the culture!

And Watch It Happen Every Day!

WHAT DID WE TAKE ON FIRST?

As I said, this was not about planning, but acting to take care of these problems.

Right off the bat, we knew we had to stop the stuff that everyone knew about, but nobody had done anything about —

> leave abuse, people coming into work late and leaving early and taking two hours for lunch...
>
> and we had to fix the overtime problems.

But we also knew **we had to stop abusive workplace behavior...**

"I'll Teach You My Job!"

We had to end the feeling that these egregiously bad employees, these just unquestionably difficult people for whatever reason —

as well as bad supervisors and managers would **never be dealt with.**

This didn't necessarily mean firing people, but it did mean that — not just me, but you — whether you're a manager, a supervisor, a division head…

or an executive group member, even the president or the CEO,

had to immerse ourselves into the inner-workings of our offices and groups and to **change the work dynamics** and relationships there.

And Watch It Happen Every Day!
___

We knew this had to be done.

It was bad enough that the "egregiously bad and difficult" employee, supervisor, or manager... was making their current colleagues unhappy and perhaps feeling hopeless about their work situation,

we had to recognize that **our allowing workplace abuse** to continue would also mean that any people we had hired —

once they started to work and then saw the internal problems of the workplace and what was not being taken care of,

some of them would not only have question their decision to join us... some might also then decide to leave because of the climate/culture...

And...

all the work we had done, the efforts we had made to bring in better people — new colleagues we had worked hard to join us — would be for naught.

But, while we realized that **it was imperative** to get at each instance of the bad/difficult employee, manager, or supervisor problem,

> it was obvious that the problem of workplace abuse was not limited to a few isolated cases...

that the approach of responding to and "fixing" each specific problem after it had occurred was like a game of **organizational "whack a mole."**

And as we were always playing "catch-up" — it became very clear that trying to deal with these egregiously bad people and situations this way was not going to work in the long-run...

And Watch It Happen Every Day!
_____

and would not lead to enduring change that would make us a better organization.

Thus, **rather than being reactive,** we realized that, if we wanted to make our organization better, what we needed an organization-wide solution...

one that was proactive.

And, without any forethought, what we found ourselves saying in doing the SWOT analysis at the retreat... was that all these problems which were repeatedly occurring...

were things we didn't like... because they were violations of our personal values and...

"I'll Teach You My Job!"

BAM!

what some of us knew... were also totally counter to what we say in policies and manuals about who we were to be!

That is, as in any organization, we **said the right things...**

> treat each other with respect, value our diversity and multi-culturalism,

be collaborative and supportive, and conduct ourselves with professionalism.

So it wasn't that these statements — these ideas and principles didn't exist. They did, but what had happened was that as an organization...

we had let lapse/never clearly established that these

And Watch It Happen Every Day!
_____

statements were what was expected of people in the workplace...

As an organization, we just **had a big hole...**

that, even though policies which should back, support, and encourage every employee, every manager, and every supervisor, every division head, and those who were executives...

across the entire organization to **do the right thing,**

our problem really was that these policies which were "on the books" — found in manuals and numerous memoranda —

had long been **"in effect but never enforced."**

I know your reaction...

Policies? Really? Enforce?

I understand that most people, including anyone reading this book, understandably can be skeptical about policies and their impact.

Far too often, our experience is that policies often "just get in the way of getting things done"... but policies, in these cases of the egregiously bad stuff,

were just logical and were what was needed...

In fact, **they were exactly what was needed!**

That is, policies — unequivocally clear statements of the

And Watch It Happen Every Day!

organization's values and expectations…

would reinforce and strengthen the behaviors and attitudes that should just be the way things are in a decent, productive place to work.

It also became clear that unless everyone,

>including executives as well as managers, supervisors, and those in our group –

>as well as anyone else wherever s/he might work in the organization,

became aware of these policies… and to know the expectations that they should adhere to, the problems of bad/difficult employees, managers, supervisors, and executives would remain.

It came down to the fact that getting better **wasn't a matter of courage —**

of feeling so aggrieved or insulted by bad behavior and attitude that one finally had to speak up and act.

Getting better — changing the culture to get rid of the egregiously bad and to make us a better place to work...

was simply a matter of consistently stating what were desired workplace norms and values,

and then to act... which was what policies enabled us to do!

That is, while they were reflective of legal requirements, policies were really statements of the ideals of the organization.

And Watch It Happen Every Day!

And as statements of expectation that could be enforced...

policies would not only express what the culture of our organization should be... and thus influence and affect what was going on in various offices and between/among people,

creating not just a decent but hopefully a highly desirable place to work.

They were also the basis to help us to remove/"subtract" or put the difficult, egregiously bad individuals in their place where their adverse attitudes and behavior would be limited/stopped.

So, we figured out which policies needed to be issued or rewritten... and keep in mind, every organization, every business has statements like these!

"I'll Teach You My Job!"

and we crafted new policies that were needed to take on these issues.

We put out a notice tied to the organization's fraud policy... and brought to everyone's attention... that anyone who was not reporting his/her sick leave and vacation leave correctly was committing fraud —

a criminal offense that might possibly lead to termination of employment and/or that the organization might choose to prosecute.

That was followed by **a "zero tolerance"** policy on workplace violence... a new policy — not to encompass just physical violence (assaults), but also psychological violence...

that **toxic, intolerable stuff** that makes people's stomach churn...

And Watch It Happen Every Day!

intimidation, speaking angrily/openly yelling at someone that some people just, for whatever reason —

perhaps their crazy notion of how to manage and lead because they were in charge, **chose to inflict** on others...

but in doing so, by behaving this way, they were making for a place where no one would want to work/would dread coming to work.

To deal with **the problem of people coming** into work late or leaving early, we sent out a memorandum reiterating the policy on organizational workhours (8 to 5).

And this workhours policy gave us the leverage to address the overtime problem.

That memorandum on overtime went out to managers/supervisors/executives and was also sent to those who work with and for you... to not ask/compel their employees —

who were on a 40-hour work week and eligible for overtime for hours worked beyond 40 hours,

to work beyond standard work hours.

Finally, I got myself as well as three others **trained to investigate incidents** and to deal with complaints.

By conducting these investigations, issuing findings, and making recommendations and tying the reports to policies,

And Watch It Happen Every Day!
_____

while we took on and resolved the specific instances of discrimination and workplace violence...

and while we were letting everyone know for perhaps the first time what the organization's policies and institutional expectations were,

the real impact was the organization's **culture was changing.**

As we started taking on these long-standing adverse practices, there was remarkably very little objection or much comment about what we were doing.

> After all, as everyone knew about these problems but with nothing being done for years,
>
> why would anyone have any expectations that what we were doing would have lasting change, that anything would be different?

"I'll Teach You My Job!"

However, we **didn't have to wait** long for our first test.

The policy changes did catch some people's eye.

And one day, a courageous employee... who had transferred from another organization could not believe that her boss —

an executive — was regularly yelling at her and others in the office. This executive had been doing this for years and even though numerous "conversations" had been held, nothing changed.

When the workplace violence policy came out, this employee **asked for an investigation.**

I conducted the investigation... a report was issued and the administrator's behavior was found to be

And Watch It Happen Every Day!
_____

unacceptable... in violation of the zero-tolerance workplace violence policy.

No one said much of anything, but **the word spread.**

The leave abuse memorandum tied to the fraud policy also caught people's attention.

No one had thought that leave abuse was really fraud — a misrepresentation where someone was receiving undeserved financial benefit!

It wasn't long before we were told about a situation in a unit where the person was alleged to have failed to report vacation and leave usage for years.

In another instance, a couple of employees had taken

"I'll Teach You My Job!"

extended time off (which was not reported) because they had worked long hours on a project.

Because the leave abuse was **tied to the organization's fraud policy,** internal audit which was responsible for issuing that policy got involved.

They conducted their investigation and issued their report, resulting in the dismissal of employees and a strong reprimand to the head of the unit.

Closer to home, I had one employee who resisted the work hour policy.

This individual would often come in late to work, dropping a child at school... and then take lunch at 11:30AM to avoid the lunch-time rush.

Leaving early for lunch was bad enough, but the person "on occasion" then didn't return to work until 1PM or

And Watch It Happen Every Day!
___

later,

when everyone else on the one-hour lunch break schedule would come back to work.

I explained the policy, enforced it by not allowing the person to leave early for lunch and the person soon found another job.

As a result of these actions, **the word got out... amazing how fast the grapevine is.**

Even in the face of a long history of things not being done or taken on, people began to sense that these challenges that had long not been addressed were no longer acceptable.

And what we were after began to happen.

"I'll Teach You My Job!"

You could sense the **organizational climate beginning to shift...**

It really didn't take long...

So, what to keep in mind?

While some/many of us who are "in charge" have had more than our share of frustrations in dealing with egregiously bad people...

a difficult employee, manager, division head, or an executive...

just I had done, **you also, by relying on policy can remove — that is, subtract** these individuals or put them in their place.

And as they will no longer be allowed to "get away" with being abusive or not being held accountable, just as we

And Watch It Happen Every Day!

were becoming that better place... you as well may find where you work becoming

the kind of place that now had a culture where people would want to come to work.

"I'll Teach You My Job!"

Book 3 — "Connecting More Than Just Dots"

Fast forward to the next year —

Operationally we've made a lot of progress — feeling pretty good about getting on top of our work...

and we've also started to successfully take on the "Dead Moose" stuff.

All pretty exciting and energizing!

We go on another retreat to step back and get perspective so we can figure out how to be better.

And Watch It Happen Every Day!

Now, I know we've all been on retreats, but what happened at **this retreat opened my eyes...**

and let me begin to see a number of things about those who worked with and for me that would make us even more effective.

I know that a retreat is a standard way to get a sense of what we need to address. They give us a chance to relax, but also focus on what we could do to improve. And for the most part, they are successful.

I have no problem with retreats. But when I did this retreat which I describe in this book where, without a plan or intent to do so, those who worked with and for me , showed that retreats can give us so much more...

We start with a team-building exercise where each of us tells our life history — what got each of us to where we are now and what were the events that helped shape our lives.

I watched in amazement as **people opened up** — they weren't just engaged in a team-building exercise. It was clear that everyone was interested in hearing about each other…

They wanted to know more about what made someone tick.

And as I watched, more than just a light bulb going on, **another lightning bolt struck!**

Because I already knew from the work we had done on operational tasks and the schedule of daily work… as well as the calendar and the "dead moose" challenges…

And Watch It Happen Every Day!
___

that these are **clearly smart people.**

And now, from these conversations at the retreat about each person's background/what they had done, I realized that...

these are also people who, in their lives, are not waiting for someone to tell them what to do,

these are people who are **shaping their own lives!**

And on the spot, I decided that each person... would be responsible for a part of the retreat — and thus help shape what we were doing.

"I'll Teach You My Job!"

To get this underway, I emphasized to each of them that they should act like they were the director, that they **were now in charge** and each would have lead responsibility for running a portion of the retreat...

> whether the environment scan, the SWOT analysis, or the determination of our priorities

to come up with the must do's and the really want to do's that we knew we had to develop!

Of course, **doing the retreat this way wasn't** even on the agenda, but after a few moments of hesitation...

> "Are you sure? Is this really what you're going to have us do?"

Their reluctance was understandable...
they had never been given the chance to be in charge at

And Watch It Happen Every Day!

work… they were used to being told what to do and to react to someone else's ideas or thoughts.

But as it became clear that I was serious in wanting them to do this, people came out of their shells and they started to change.

In fact, some really jumped at the opportunity — and to be honest…

some like Lola expressed such strong opinions and recommendations — they shocked most of us with the directness of what they'd do (actually demand) in changing things.

But, as difficult as this was to run the retreat this way, **the light began to go on** in my head and I came to realize…

if we were to come up with what we needed to work on, it was critical to hear what people were really thinking... what they thought we should do.

Of course, with not all people being the same, as the various discussions proceeded,

those who had not spoken up initially... **found their voices** and asked questions that needed to be asked and shared powerful insights.

It was surprising to hear how much they knew... And then those who were usually more demanding and insistent that their point of view was right,

instead of ordering and trying to be in control (that is, "directing"), they did what they did in the daily meetings — what they knew had worked...

And Watch It Happen Every Day!

they began to share why they had a particular view, to ask for input, to seek out the thoughts and views of others.

And as they did this, the demanding ones came to realize that as a manager, "you really do have to get work done through others,"

and the others **responded positively and delivered!**

So, the retreat tells/helps us see what's not working operationally, and where we are on the egregiously bad "dead moose" challenges,

and that we have also begun to develop a sense of what to work on to make us as well as the organization better.

"I'll Teach You My Job!"

All of which, of course, was good...

But the best thing that came out of the retreat was that we learned... more like "had stumbled upon" —

that having each person lead a part of the retreat was a **"better way"** to pull out concerns and develop solutions to move us forward!

While what we did at the retreat was entirely new, and while we got a much better sense of what we had to take on, we also learned two other important things:

FIRST, what we came away with — drawn from the environment scan and the SWOT analysis... was not our goals, which is the standard outcome of strategic planning, but...

And Watch It Happen Every Day!

---

a solid list of important projects to work on.

These projects became our focus for change... "By the end of X — the calendar year, summer, three months, or whatever timeframe."

Grouping these projects together around the theme — **"What We Wanted to Look Like,"**

we never even talked about goals! We only talked about what we needed to do to take us to the next level/something of desired change...

and by the end of the retreat, we knew these projects would also enable our office to further move the organization to a better place.

"I'll Teach You My Job!"

As I said, as a beginning manager, **I knew about goals** from previous strategic planning efforts,

but what these retreats — which we did every year thereafter to come up with the list of items of "What We Wanted to Look Like" —

did was to shift us to come up with what was really important... **"concrete deliverables!"**

We weren't spending our time and tying up our heads working toward some "pie-in-the-sky" goals... some aspirational vision of a future.

What we were working on... were things that would have direct, positive, and immediate impact on the daily

And Watch It Happen Every Day!

work we had to do...

and also on what was going on in offices, with our colleagues, and across the organization.

So, we're **making huge strides operationally** because we're now working together collaboratively,

and we're also effective in taking on these long-standing egregious problems that would change the culture,

And now through the retreat we're creating those concrete deliverables that would provide a forward focus of change in the organization.

"I'll Teach You My Job!"

And when we came back to work, we put all of this into the calendar and daily schedule.

And we did so with the same structure —

> the full cycle of deadlines, preparation and organizational activities, materials to develop, events and meetings to be scheduled, mailings and communications

the tasks to make this all happen... as well as the follow-up to make sure we had done what we said we needed to do, and who was responsible for what.

And so that we would be reminded every day, we put all we had come up with — the "What We Wanted to Look Like" —

And Watch It Happen Every Day!

on the board in the common work area where we met **so we could see them every day!**

It was pretty surprising how things came together — how what had seemed disconnected had just become connected...

our roles and relationships, these projects for concrete deliverables... and how we organized ourselves now just fit together!

Of course, not surprisingly... just as how we ran the retreat had changed, **our meetings also changed.**

We not only had an expanded calendar/schedule with initiatives related to policy/culture/climate... we also

"I'll Teach You My Job!"

had the addition of the "concrete deliverables" tied to items in the list of "What We Wanted to Look Like."

And seeing we had much more to take on, we also changed how we did our daily work —

changing our jobs to match our processes and to assure the efficient development of the initiatives and concrete deliverable projects.

And as we also all now knew what each other was doing — the full range of each other's work — and with everyone pretty much having the same or complementary jobs...

we were working so collaboratively that **we ended the handing-off** of work and the "dizzying whirligig" of moving documents from one person to another.

And Watch It Happen Every Day!

That is, with each person or a group being assigned as a point of contact and handling the work we were expected to do... for employees and managers in a set of offices or groups in a particular area of the organization...

we were no longer handing off work which minimized the delays caused by the fragmentation of work.

We also found that, as we no longer had the problem of losing paperwork, amazingly, things **abruptly stopped dropping** through the cracks!

We had simply become faster and better at getting done what had to be done!

We had connected a lot of dots — the operational, culture and policy, the challenges, the "What We Wanted to Look Like" and the concrete deliverables — and what we got was much more complete… whole pictures of what people wanted…

and what situations, problems, and challenges were occurring and what we had to take on to make things better in the organization.

As we were taking on a lot, to keep us on track with all we were working on as well as our daily work,

we brought on board the first multi-user relational database… and used it to track every piece of paper that came into our office.

And Watch It Happen Every Day!
_____

We knew when the document came in and who it went to… who was working on what.

> We also knew when something was passed on to someone else and who that person was and the disposition of the document.

Through all of this, not only did we come to know even better what each other was doing, we came to know how what each of us was doing fit together…

and nearly **magically to also support one another.**

And without much effort or difficulty, when someone was overburdened or was absent, it was easy for someone else to stand in and pick up each other's work nearly seamlessly.

And in doing so, we ended the complaints that had haunted this office for years — that we were incompetent, that we were losing things,

that we didn't know what we were talking about and that we couldn't be trusted to do our jobs to serve our colleagues!

Again, all good, but best of all,

as important as the concrete deliverables and our working together and changing our image and the perception of our effectiveness was...

as a workgroup, we also got that SECOND insight which was something even more important.

And Watch It Happen Every Day!

What we brought back from the retreat... and as we reorganized how we did our work,

we came to acknowledge/to realize with even more conviction that... **each person was fully capable of leading...**

and the twice-weekly meetings evolved to where each person would be in charge — just as we had done at the retreat — on a rotating basis

and would run these meetings around **our symbolically square table with no head!**

This capacity to lead — which was always there in each person — became a huge strength of the group!

"I'll Teach You My Job!"

___

None of this had happened because someone had a grand scheme — a plan or some notion of what a great operation or an office should look like...

or how a group of people could really make things happen.

For sure, **it happened because...**

I knew as the manager that the standard way of doing things,

an occasional staff meeting and "my being the person in charge"... and having the "authority to lead" from the typical list of manager responsibilities, was not working.

But it happened for other reasons as well.

And Watch It Happen Every Day!

It also happened because I had that vision of that group back in Tokyo where I had worked.

It happened because I was fortunate enough to **somehow wake up and realize** that the people I was working with were amazingly smart...

that because these were people who were shaping their own lives, and who knew their jobs better than I ever would,

that they would have the insight to enable them to make crucial contributions... to figure out and do what was necessary for us to be successful.

It happened because I realized...

that they knew the problems in their jobs that stymied what each person as well as what the group was being tasked to accomplish better than I ever would,

and that **they also knew the solutions...** but what they knew had never been tapped into before.

It happened because somehow that lightning bolt — which made me realize that everyone has the capacity to lead, something they had in their own personal lives —

also made me realize that I only needed to stop thinking I was solely responsible for being in charge...

and that they would **step up and deliver,**

And Watch It Happen Every Day!
___

In response to a problem, I would offer a solution and put it on the table.

Invariably people would come back with a different and better solution!

That they would come back with better solutions wasn't surprising. As they knew their jobs better than I would ever know, why shouldn't they have a better way?

And then, when they had finished explaining their better approach, they liked to say back to me something I had told them — a saying I learned in Japan,

"There are many ways to climb Mt. Fuji..." and we'd all laugh...

----

and would do so **with an amazing synergy** that made us all more effective and productive.

"I'll Teach You My Job!"

Again, having dealt with the operational, the egregiously bad, and developing a sense of the concrete deliverables, it would be easy to now also stop at this point.

Clearly the group had become highly effective...

and, while the development of each person's capacity to lead was essential to our daily work to continue to address the organizational challenges of culture and climate...

but now to also develop a much better sense of what our work ahead was going to be —

>that is, the concerns falling into "What We Wanted to Look Like," to move our group, our division and even the organization really forward,

we realized that putting initiatives together and developing the concrete deliverables was not easy to do.

And Watch It Happen Every Day!

___

We realized that if we were to be successful... **doing so would take longer-range,** more complex and overarching thinking and organizing.

It meant we had to plan and to plan well, it meant... **we had to manage!**

We knew we had the capacity to lead — which happened through the retreat,

but if we —

including myself who began by struggling to figure out what I was to do in this job... what I would do as a manager —

and this group of people, most of whom really had not held formal management responsibilities —

now had to manage,

the obvious question that loomed... the question that needed answering was, were we ready?

Could we take what we knew from leading and managing/shaping our own lives and leverage that to move us forward at work?

And Watch It Happen Every Day!

Book 4.1 — "Realizing What It Takes"

Developing a capacity to manage was critical since neither I nor those in our group had been managers who had been highly effective.

And now, with us as a group **striving to** develop concrete deliverables, there was no question…

that it was **imperative to figure out the best way to manage** to take on the work of developing these new initiatives.

"I'll Teach You My Job!"

----

*This Book 4.1 and the following two books **are controversial. They depart from conventional wisdom...***

If you're an established manager, you might find some/considerable disagreement with what I write because, after all, you've been able to do your job of managing with decent if not solid results for a number of years.

I can't argue with that view.

However, I want to give you something to think about.

Just because the NY Yankees from the 30's to the 60's were world champions of baseball numerous times didn't mean that they would continue to be successful — to dominate the game of baseball.

In fact, we know they didn't. Other teams became quite good — Milwaukee, Boston, Baltimore, Brooklyn, Atlanta — and later Houston and Los Angeles as well as Chicago, St. Louis, and Cleveland regularly fielded highly competitive championship teams. The Yankees remained decently competitive but no longer dominant.

And Watch It Happen Every Day!

And why not? Was it possibly related to less than stellar management and leadership? Perhaps an organization that wasn't working quite right? Or decisions that were made which turned out to be not on target if not flat-out wrong? Or did they somehow stand still with what they thought was a proven formula while other teams changed and became outstanding?

And to get back to this book and our focus on businesses and organizations...

Keep in mind that only five companies of those that constitute the Dow-Jones Industrial Average were part of the Dow in 1975 — Exxon, Procter and Gamble, DuPont, United Technologies, and 3M. GE, the last member of the original DOW group, was dropped in 2018. Additionally, over 50% of the companies listed in the Fortune 500 have been replaced since the early 2000s.

Was management a factor in the decline/failure of those companies?

"I'll Teach You My Job!"

And as I'm pondering what to do, this guy named **ElRoy Face suddenly popped** into my mind!

Wow... total surprise! ElRoy Face??

What possible connection could ElRoy Face — a baseball pitcher in the 50's and 60's — have to our managing challenge?

But, as ElRoy Face wouldn't disappear from my thoughts, one afternoon, **it hit me!**

We all know that **some people** are great managers; however, we also know they are **few and far between.**

And Watch It Happen Every Day!

Then there are some/many of us who fall in the middle group. We're decent... we're ok... we do what we need to do to try to get the job done.

But for most of what we do, we're not extraordinary, and being in the middle group, it means **we're at best average...**

And, of course, there are a few of us who are struggling.

So, what does that have to do with ElRoy Face?

A lot...

As a minor league pitcher, ElRoy Face was quite successful.

"I'll Teach You My Job!"

Over five seasons, opposing teams were held to the equivalent of less than 4 runs per game...

and he compiled a won-lost record of 69 and 27, a winning percentage of 72% or nearly 3 out of every four games he pitched.

However, when he was brought up to the major league team, the Pittsburgh Pirates, for the 1953 season,

the hitters on the opposing teams were able to hit his pitching, and his run allowed per game average nearly doubled, rising to nearly 7 runs per game.

And during those first five years of his major league career with the Pirates, ElRoy Face was doing okay,

but his won-lost record fell to 32 wins and 36 losses, with a winning percentage of 47% or about average.

And Watch It Happen Every Day!

But **suddenly** in 1959, he did something that was simply extraordinary.

Unexpectedly... and **to the amazement** of the entire baseball world, a guy who had been a pitcher with an average record...

did the exceptional feat that no one else had done before!

ElRoy Face won 18 games and lost only one!

ElRoy Face started his major league career in 1953, but not with great success. And in his first season (1953) his RA9 (runs allowed adjusted to 9 innings) was 6.81. This

"I'll Teach You My Job!"

means if he pitched a full nine innings, nearly 7 runs a game would be scored by the opposing team when he was the pitcher.

As this RA9 was too high, he was told to develop another pitch. So, in 1954, he developed the forkball...

And for the next six seasons (1955-1960) with Pittsburgh, he remarkably reduced his RA9 from nearly 7 to 4.15, 3.79, 3.94, 3.23, 2.80 (1959), and 3.06. Of note, in his career, he had five seasons when his RA9 was below 3.00.

In talking with ElRoy Face about his pitching prowess, he took particular pride in the fact that he had pitched in 9 straight games which is beyond what nearly any other pitcher could do! Because of the stress on their arms caused by the violent act of throwing the ball oftentimes upwards of 90 miles per hour, pitchers usually require at least two if not three days of rest to recover between the games they would pitch. Face pitched in 17 innings across those 9 games.

And Watch It Happen Every Day!

And in compiling **the best winning** percentage of 94.7% for a pitcher in the history of baseball,

he changed the way the game is played!

So how did Face go from being average to extraordinary?

Simple: He changed what he was doing as a pitcher... and threw the ball in a different way that no one else in major league baseball was doing...

And when Face threw his forkball, it was a pitch that most hitters found difficult to hit!

"I'll Teach You My Job!"

Of course, **Face captivated** the baseball world, **becoming known as the first "closer"** in the game of baseball...

a pitcher who would come into the game in the late innings to shut down the other team.

And by having such great success capped by his 18-win 1-loss season in 1959,

thus forcing other baseball teams to develop their own specialized relief pitchers to compete against him in the late innings of a baseball game,

ElRoy Face changed the way the game is played!

And Watch It Happen Every Day!

COMING TO GRIPS WITH MANAGING

So, nice story about ElRoy Face, but **what possible connection** does this have to do with managing?

The success of ElRoy Face tells us, whether we're a manager, a supervisor, a director, or an executive...

while there are reasons why we fall short and even fail at times...

there are also **things we can do to optimize** our chances of being successful!

And, as I thought about my own career and why I was a struggling manager, **I had some important breakthroughs**...

"I'll Teach You My Job!"

that led me to understand what wasn't working and helped put my head in the right place and what I had to change.

It started with... despite all we've read and been told,

the simple fact is that we're not trained for success... we're trained to be average.

Wait! Stop!

And Watch It Happen Every Day!
___

We're not trained for success? How did you come up with that?

I thought about the jobs I had held and I also talked with many others who were in management.

If you asked whether **the jobs we held** were the same as previous jobs we had, we all would say they were similar, but not the same...

> different organizations, different businesses, different activities, different priorities, different responsibilities.

All true, but then I thought:

"I'll Teach You My Job!"

Even though the jobs were different, when any of us got into a new position, **did we bring** what we had done previously to our current jobs?

Of course!

No one starts anew. **We bring** what we thought worked in our previous jobs and try to use that in our new jobs!

So, then I thought, if we say that…"as a manager in a new job, most of us continue to use what we had used in our previous jobs…"

even though we all know that the problems aren't the same and the work as well as supporting systems/processes are not the same…

isn't that a problem?

And Watch It Happen Every Day!
_____

In response people said,

Well, because the job is new, we know that we're going to **have to learn** some things about our new place of work if we're to be successful.

And again, as that made total sense...

I asked, "What did you do? What did your organization or business do?"

Nearly everyone said that, as a new manager or supervisor, they got sent to a new manager or supervisor training session...

and some also got sent to a leadership development program (upper management, executives) that the organization had put together!

And when I asked, "What did you learn? Did you **find the session helpful?"**

People replied that, while there was some new information about the organization or the company,

these sessions — regardless of the organization or company — **were pretty much the same.**

Well organized, but they covered much of what we **already knew:**

a vision/mission that gave an overview, followed by information on hiring, performance management, communication, mentoring and coaching, and

And Watch It Happen Every Day!

compliance.

So, because we've all gone through these programs at previous places we had worked and thus already know a lot about these topics,

I came to an important realization.

As there's nothing really new in these programs, **they don't make you better.**

And the reason they don't... is because the information/training being provided which all attending the workshop are expected to understand and use — is the same, and **by targeting all managers** with the same content, these workshops simply can't be responsive to what you or I — as managers with **our unique situations, issues, and problems** — have to deal with!

And then that big, glaring light bulb went on!

What any manager really wants is the information I/you need to be effective in our work...

and in order to do that — in order to make a difference... to provide better service, faster and

And Watch It Happen Every Day!

improved operations, to assure production of goods and products...

to create the conditions for stronger performance by everyone,

what we have to focus on... are the problems, issues, and challenges that are **unique to the work** we're doing!

Repeat! If we — meaning myself and those in my group — are to be effective,

what we have to focus on are the problems, issues, and challenges that are unique to the work we are doing!

For, if we handle those effectively, we will provide precisely what our customers and clients want and/or need!

If it were simply a matter of bringing what we'd done previously — and combining it with what we learned in training,

each time we took on a new position, **we'd build** on what we know, adding what we've just learned... and be on an **ever upward-moving path** of greater and greater success!

But we know that **ever-escalating success** doesn't happen... because what we've been told is not specific to the office or work group that we're in charge of.

And because we received the same information — information many of us already had and information

And Watch It Happen Every Day!

that's not about the problems, issues, and challenges we have to take care of, we don't become better in the work we're responsible for.

And, since we just don't really improve, **I came to realize** that what these workshops do... in laying out what the organization expects of all managers,

is to pretty much bring everyone **to the same decent level** of management.

And thus, not only should we not be surprised that so many of us are just decent, average managers...

we also shouldn't be surprised that **we achieve similar level (meaning average) of results!**

"I'll Teach You My Job!"
___

And what directly follows is... because I and most of you were trained to be average,

and not sufficiently trained to manage and lead in handling the real problems and issues that I and those working with and for me had to deal with every day...

those daily operational problems and the egregious challenges of "bad employees, colleagues and administrators" within our offices or groups.

it should also not come as a surprise that I...

that many of us who are managers **would fall short...**

And Watch It Happen Every Day!

---

couldn't be superbly effective!

It was this realization through these conversations with many other managers about their careers — and also by reflecting on my own career...

that led me to understand that the standard approach to managing **won't achieve fabulous results.**

And, just like that... I suddenly understood — like ElRoy Face who understood that he had to change to pitch effectively,

"I'll Teach You My Job!"

why making a change — **a change, whether we're a baseball pitcher or a manager...**

to focus on what we had to do in our daily work...

is what's needed to enable us to be highly successful in all that we were undertaking!

And Watch It Happen Every Day!

Book 4.2 — "Coming Together on Managing"

Once I realized that we were not being trained — whether formally or informally — to be extraordinary, that we weren't being trained for success,

I had another piece of **unconventional wisdom about managing** pop into my mind!

And this second perspective will seem a little strange…

I've just written that we're all trained to be average — that we pretty much end up being average managers.

"I'll Teach You My Job!"

But now I'm going to talk about **how each of us is unique!**

Wait! That's confusing!

You just made an argument in the previous book that we're all the same and now you're going to say that we're unique?

Exactly!

There are obvious reasons why **each of us is unique...**

And Watch It Happen Every Day!
___

We have different personalities — some of us are low-key, others view being inspiring as our strength, some of us are more driven, and others are more approachable.

In addition, we have different skills and knowledge…

like budgeting, running a team of machine tool operators, or being a pilot in charge of a flight crew on a commercial airliner…

All of which, without question, **make each of us different.**

However, while all of these unique characteristics make us different from one another,

there is **one unique characteristic that's true across every one of us…**

and it's true whether we think we're a fabulous manager or if we are struggling and **aren't a great manager:**

AND THAT COMMON CHARACTERISTIC IS:

Each of us knows our job better than anyone else!

Repeat: Each of us knows our job better than anyone else!

And Watch It Happen Every Day!

Think about it.

Do you think your boss knows your job?

If he/she had to step in and do the work you do or the work that I do,

most of us would say, with perhaps an exception of two, that **the person we report to would not be able to do our jobs...**

And the reason is that our bosses — whether yours or mine — really don't know what we do.

And if that's the case,

if someone wants to know how you manage, or supervise or do your job as the CEO,

"I'll Teach You My Job!"

---

there's no one better to ask than you!

HOWEVER, THEN ANOTHER INSIGHT...

While it's good that we are the ones to turn to because we know our jobs the best,

I then had **some sobering thoughts** that followed:

Just as **no one knows your** job as well as you do and your boss can't do your job,

And Watch It Happen Every Day!

do you really know the jobs of each of the people who is in your group?

Can you do their jobs?

Just as your boss would struggle to do your job...

> because he/she doesn't know what you do every day,

isn't it likely that you would also struggle doing the job of someone reporting to you...

because you don't know what that person has to do every day?

So, following from not knowing the jobs of those who work for us...

again, the parallel to our bosses not being able to do our jobs,

I had this next thought which prompted a rethinking about the way most of us manage — which, if it is correct,

can move us from being at best average to **highly effective!**

THE CONSEQUENCES OF THE MINDSET OF BEING "IN CHARGE"

And Watch It Happen Every Day!

As we all know, in the standard approach to managing that we've all learned, one of the main underlying but unstated ideas about what managers do...

is that when you're the manager — or a supervisor or an executive — **you are in charge.**

Every boss I've worked for over the years thinks this way...

It's just **one of the long-standing** norms in organizational life — the way things are.

"I'm in charge because I — and those who put me in this job, think that I should be... And, as **I obviously know something** or a lot of things that others don't,

"I'll Teach You My Job!"

I know best,

and, in knowing the best, I'm therefore **the one best- suited to lead** and manage and to make decisions that gets results."

However, is this idea that someone is in charge because the person knows better/best **really on target?**

While some of you may answer "yes,"

that you do know "better" — that **you can make better** decisions... and have greater insight as to what is to be done — and even how to do it,

And Watch It Happen Every Day!

think back to that question posed a few pages earlier.

Can you do the job of someone reporting to you?

Even if some of us would say that we can... if that question is somewhat representative of how we can demonstrate that we "know better" — then here's **the tougher question:**

Would you then extend that and say that you can also do the jobs... of two perhaps even three or more individuals who are employees in your office or work group?

Can you do the jobs of all of them better than all of them combined?

Of course, you can't.

"I'll Teach You My Job!"

If you could, you could do all of their work and **you wouldn't need them.**

Now, I know what you're thinking… The reason you need them is because there's so much work to do… that you by yourself can't do it all — even though you know more and have more skills and/or knowledge.

But here's what I concluded:

The reason **we can't do** the jobs of everyone and can't do them better than all of them combined is… because **we really don't know** the detail of the work they do…

And Watch It Happen Every Day!

just as your boss doesn't know the detail of your work!

And therefore, as managers, don't we have to accept the fact that **they know a heck of a lot** —

and that, despite my believing I'm in charge — I really don't know their jobs better than they do.

That if it is the case for them to do their work every day, **they really do know better** — they have to know their jobs better than I ever would...

because if they didn't,

> and because — whether it's you or me — we don't know their jobs well enough to do in their jobs,

"I'll Teach You My Job!"

things wouldn't get done.

So, just as you **know your job better** than your boss,

and those who work with and for me/you also know more about what needs to be done and how to do it better than any of us as managers will ever know...

shouldn't we accept that how we've been trained and learned to manage doesn't really work?

While these insights helped me enormously as a manager... turning me around,

And Watch It Happen Every Day!

there is **one final piece** we need to talk about — an important piece that gets to the **challenge of managing effectively.**

THE QUESTION ABOUT MANAGING THAT NEEDS TO BE ANSWERED

Just as your boss doesn't know your job...

and you don't know the jobs of the people who work with and for you...

do you think those who **work for you know your job?**

Repeat: Do you think **they know your job?**

"I'll Teach You My Job!"

The answer is... not likely!

Because we're in charge and we know best, how **could they possibly know** or understand what we do?

So, here's what all of this leads to:

When you don't know the job of the person you report to... and that person doesn't know your job...

and when you don't know the jobs of the people who work with and for you

and the people working with and for you don't know your job,

And Watch It Happen Every Day!
_____

it's pretty likely that what we are doing is going to be sub-optimal...

that we're not going to do a good job individually and as a group!

So, **if collectively we** don't really know what each other is doing, can we say, as the managers who "are in charge" **that we are managing well?**

If you find it difficult to explain your job...

> because we have so longed relied upon the conventional wisdom...

> that a manager (or a supervisor or an executive) is in charge and knows best,

and that therefore the people who work with and for you

most **certainly don't need** to know what you do or have the knowledge of skill to do your job,

the reality is that **they can't know** your job.

So, once again, **because they don't know** your job, can you expect them to really do what you think is important?

Now, I know many of us would say.

"They'll know what's important **because I will tell** them what I have decided is important for them to do."

And Watch It Happen Every Day!
_____

But knowing that the standard management practice of organizing and directing by and large **has generated average results**,

what is the likelihood that this assumption of being in charge,

>where you plan and organize and tell others what you think is important

>and where how you've been trained results in your being average —

is going to lead to **astounding success?**

And when you have sat back and thought about all of the above... **THE POINTS OF THIS BOOK 4.1**

"I'll Teach You My Job!"

1. that I know my job better than anyone else,

2. that my boss can't do my job because s/he doesn't know what I do every day,

3. that I don't know the jobs of people who work for me,

4. and that the people who report to me don't know my job...

can you still say that you know better?

That you are as effective a manager as you could be?

And Watch It Happen Every Day!

Books 5 through 8

"If You've Not Gotten the Results You Expected…

Book 5 — "Adults!" The Breakthrough to Managing Well

Book 6 — "You Can't Change People. You Can Only Change the Way You Work with Them "

Book 7 — The Book Specifically for Those of Us "Who Are in Charge"

Book 8 — The Twice-Weekly Meetings… Some Hold Them Every Day or Twice-a Day

Book 5 — "Adults!" The Breakthrough to Managing Well

First, on the upside...

As the manager, I had learned what the people who worked with and for me were doing.

But more importantly, **as those individuals** in the group had also learned what each other was doing on a daily basis,

they all become more coordinated and collaborative as well as faster in their work and therefore more productive and effective.

But, despite all of these developments that any manager would want to see happen,

And Watch It Happen Every Day!

I found that there was a troubling downside for me as the manager.

If the management practices and approaches which have long shaped our careers as managers... **instead of accelerating my success,** had made me average,

and at the same time, if those who worked with and for me did not know my job...

and if I myself didn't know on a daily basis what I was doing that was directly related to and had direct impact on their work,

yet the group had made major progress,

"I'll Teach You My Job!"

I realized I had to face **a serious question...**

Exactly what was I doing/should be doing in my job that would make a difference and would contribute significantly to the productivity and success that was occurring?

Of course, **the easy answer is to say** that I should change my role...

But, having learned to manage by those long-standing concepts of managing, I had no sense of what I would do differently as a manager.

Now, I know some might say, there's a lot out there about what managers should be doing. To become a better, more impactful manager,

And Watch It Happen Every Day!
___

focus on supporting the people doing the work...

- **Be a positive, proactive, and encouraging** person who is always available;

- work collaboratively with each employee to come to mutual agreement about what training and goals to pursue;

- hold periodic meetings — "one-on-ones" — to check on progress and to provide advice;

- be a coach and a mentor.

But having tried those things over many years, I know that for most of us, they don't really work.

They feel forced — sometimes like we're going through the motions;

they're also uncomfortable to varying degrees for both myself as well as the employee when we get together.

I also felt that it was hard to be consistent…

I might say one thing to one employee and in forgetting to also say that to others, there was some confusion which I'd have to spend time straightening out…

and, frankly, **few of us really have the time** to get the training we need to do these activities well.

But what was most troubling…

And Watch It Happen Every Day!

was that I realized these were activities that I didn't have the time/wasn't able to do every day.

And if I were to have impact on the daily activities being done by those who worked with and for me, I needed to figure out what I would be doing to work with them every day,

Repeat: Every day…

Of course, I then spent a great deal of time thinking about my role…

And then one day, **BAM!**

I had two thoughts pop into my head…
and things became clear, logical, and just made sense.

"I'll Teach You My Job!"

THE FIRST RETHINKING:

I realized what I was looking for...

that is, the best way to proceed that would lead to impactful change on my work... had always been right in front of me!

It had surfaced through the discussions with my colleagues at our retreats,

but at the time — **because we were caught up** in the excitement of change,

I didn't pick up on it.

And Watch It Happen Every Day!

What came to me was... I realized who these people were who were working with and for me...

and that it didn't matter... whether it was the records clerk, the receptionist, the person handling technology, or a someone in a professional capacity,

it was simply remarkable that all of them were able to step up and take on what I had asked them to do at the retreat which,

if you thought about it, under the circumstances of no preparation or introduction,

what they had achieved at the retreat and after we returned to work was amazing!

And as I thought about what I had seen that they were able to do, I got a simply remarkable insight…

a mind-opening perspective which enabled me to understand how to look at my job and most importantly our relationship.

So, bear with me as I get at this somewhat indirectly.

All of us have heard the following:

"Good managers get things done through others"

and, of course, as managers we like this phrase and think it's great because it infers/indirectly compliments us…

And Watch It Happen Every Day!

that we are good managers because we had the smarts to make things happen/that need to be done!

And the reason things got done was that we hired the people who were productive and effective and took care of the work they were supposed to do.

But, again, as those working for and with me had become highly productive, but I had remained average,

is it really accurate to say that I was a "good manager"?... A manager who really had made all of this happen?

"I'll Teach You My Job!"

The reality was that it was because everyone now knew on a daily basis what each person was doing — today, tomorrow, this week and the next...

and were working with greater collaboration —

and not what I was doing as a manager **was why they had become more productive and effective!**

And having this realization led to something more important!

As I thought back to those retreats and when I asked them to take over parts of the retreat,

the question was... why were they able to step up and take on those responsibilities?

And Watch It Happen Every Day!

"I then had another "AHA!" moment!

What had happened was that each person... whether it was Debbie, Melissa, Albert, and others, had undertaken activities to lead and to manage.

And, as they had done this well and with enthusiasm... and I, as the manager, had not trained, coached, or mentored them to do this,

I realized that their doing so brought into question whether another piece of management lore...

>which framed the way that we in nearly every organization or business have long looked at people, meaning those who we call our employees —

but in effect misleads and keeps us from seeing who those who worked with and for me/us were...

And what was that long-standing concept?

Something most of us don't think about... maybe don't even know because it is not commonly discussed, but is universally used and is highly impactful...

"The employer-employee contract!"

The employer-employee contract?

Just think about how we go about hiring people.

And Watch It Happen Every Day!

We use a particular frame of mind that influences how we view those who report to us...

Because we hired people, and they have agreed to do a certain job or work in return for a salary or hourly pay,

we've created an employment contract or an agreement to which anyone we've hired has agreed,

where we, as the employer, have the right/the authority to tell them what to do and in return we will pay them for the work that they do.

All of which is reasonable...

but, given what had happened at the retreat as well as in our daily work, if we were working in the framework of "the employer-employee contract,"

"I'll Teach You My Job!"

---

how were they able to lead their part of the retreat and also resolve many of the issues that had been limiting out effectiveness if they were "just employees" and I hadn't told them what to do or how to do it?

And, **as I tried to "come to grips"** with the dilemma of how those who were "just employees" were able to be on target and help us make the right changes,

I realized that the employer-employee mindframe, combined with the idea that it's because we're "good managers" that things are getting done,

had had a subtle but substantial adverse effect on how we work with those who work with and for us.

And Watch It Happen Every Day!

And, as the consequences of working under this assumption about this essential relationship,

where, as long as we see them as employees and that we're in charge as the employer,

we won't see that people of necessity must in fact also engage in managing….

just as they had done at the retreat and now in becoming more productive.

And why we won't see that they do manage is because, as I said in the previous book, we as managers, as supervisors, directors, or executives…

simply aren't working close enough

with them every day to see what they're doing,

and without knowing the detail of what they do in their work, we won't realize — not only do they know their jobs better than you and me as managers ever will…

that, in order to get their work done, **they simply have to "self-manage!"**

Repeat: They simply have to self-manage!

Thus, even though we say, "Good managers get things done through people," it's very unlikely that what needs to happen will occur at the levels we'd like… so long as we have a relationship based on the employer-employee contract.

And Watch It Happen Every Day!

But the fact that it occurred when these individuals rose to the occasion at the retreat and when we returned to work...

said that mindset was flawed/was a problem.

Now, I understand if you're a manager or a supervisor or an executive who has had success that you might not agree, so I want to give you a quick example to drive the point home.

Just think again about your own job...

Isn't it also the case, because your boss doesn't know your job better than you do,

"I'll Teach You My Job!"

that you also have to "self-manage" to do your job!

So, if the first rethinking is realizing that people have to "self-manage,"

What was the second rethinking?

THE "BAM" OF THE MISSING PIECE!

So, what to do to make the right leveraging change in my role as a manager?

Rethink who these people are who work with and for us... and see them for who they are!

And Watch It Happen Every Day!

Demalla, Elena, Don, Polly, Luke, Jason, Julio, Lonelle, and others… those who worked with and for me were not employees.

As I saw that they could step up and do what was necessary when I asked them, they were able to do this… not because they're employees…

they were able to do what we/they did because of who they are…

And who they are… are "Adults!"

And just like that, this missing piece – this second rethinking…

of seeing everyone as Adults — and not as employees — suddenly led to everything falling into place.

They are "Adults" not employees.

And as Adults, every day before they came to work and after they go home,

they manage, they must manage their lives and their households!

So, if people have this capacity to self-manage — "shaping their own lives," should we realize that we're making an error?

We are not talking about employees, "we are talking about Adults."

And Watch It Happen Every Day!
___

Once I saw that it was in being adults in their own lives where they got this immense capacity to lead and to manage that was essential to doing their work so well...

and that they didn't somehow magically acquire that amazing capacity to do their jobs,

but that they came to their jobs with it!

For sure, they didn't get it from us as managers since in our own mind, we're in charge and our job is to plan, organize, assess, and adjust...

And because it is their job to do what we tell them, **we never think** to teach them so they know what we do — that is, teach them our jobs as managers.

"I'll Teach You My Job!"

However, when we see our people as adults, **we do a mindshift...**

We are not talking about employees who need to be told what to do.

After all, we've already acknowledged that **they know their** jobs better than any of us as managers will ever know.

So, as we are talking about are people who, outside of work, in their own personal lives are planning, executing, assessing, and adjusting

and juggling all kinds of important balls all the time to shape their own lives...

And Watch It Happen Every Day!

this was an important realization — **a BIG BAM!**

As adults, they are fully capable of doing major important things in their lives — of making decisions.

That on a daily basis they are deciding where to invest their time and money and energy.

They know the challenges that they and their families face, what the priorities are, what must be dealt with, and how to get things done.

These are adults who are constantly assessing their current state... and figuring out the resources they have

"I'll Teach You My Job!"

or need and their capacity to achieve desired outcomes...

to purchase a home,

where to send their kids for education,

how to leverage their income for the important things in their lives.

We are talking about people who also are leaders in their churches and other organizations, who coach kids in little league teams, who organize fund-raising events for worthy causes,

and who serve as volunteers for health fairs, neighborhood cleanups and the like.

To do these things, people have to have
tremendous management skills... to

And Watch It Happen Every Day!

manage their own lives — to make adjustments to get things done — on a daily basis.

And for those of us who are managers, supervisors, executives **here's what we need to understand.**

Just as they know the challenges at home — the things that need to be dealt with and overcome, **they also know the challenges at work.**

They know what's not working — they know what's making their work difficult... and they also **have some pretty good ideas** as to what needs to be done to make things better!

So, here are the major points of this book:

1: We know that our experience as managers has not been hugely successful; that it's been pretty average...

and even though we've been taught and told that we're in charge,

because we don't know the jobs of our people and thus can't do their jobs,

don't we have to face the fact that, we, as managers, may well end up making decisions and telling people what to do that may then be off-target?

We know that the history of business and organizations has some many examples where CEO's and Presidents — those "in charge" — made bad decisions and companies

And Watch It Happen Every Day!

collapsed....

2: But, if we have a workforce — people who are really "Adults" who manage and lead in their personal lives, and they do this every day,

doesn't it make sense that our organizations and our own productivity as managers will be strengthened...

if those very talents can be **brought to bear** on a daily basis at work where they are spending eight or more hours every day?

Again,

as they know the challenges at work and we also know they have ideas that will make things better (more productive, more effective),

shouldn't we conclude that just because we're taught that we're in charge,

> where we operate in the "employer-employee" mindset and therefore think we have the responsibility to make decisions and tell people what to do,

that not only may we **be off-target,**

we might come to understand why there is a disconnect between what we say as managers and the execution of work that people do.

3: It all comes down to what I said earlier:

And Watch It Happen Every Day!

The fact is that **they also know their jobs better** than anyone else…

and just as our bosses don't know our jobs and they couldn't do them,

we can't do the jobs of our employees because we really don't know what they do.

So, in order **to do their jobs,** people have to lead and manage on their own.

4: Once we recognize that they do engage in leading and managing to do their jobs well… once we understand that people got that capacity to lead and manage…

"I'll Teach You My Job!"

because they are adults who are **shaping their own** lives outside of work — with their families, children, friends, and communities —

and once we realize that there are adverse consequences to thinking that we have the sole responsibility to make decisions and to tell people what to do because we're in charge,

we might come to understand that how we have managed, where leading and managing are set aside as responsibilities of those in charge...

with tenuous ties at best to the daily execution of work,

again, because managers do not have a clear grasp of the work people must do every day -

And Watch It Happen Every Day!

is an artificial distinction that is there every day...

that is a distinction that is nearly insurmountable to overcome... which cannot help but inhibit our effectiveness and productivity.

5: How we manage and have organized to do our work — based on long-standing concepts of managing

does not serve us well.

In fact, it assures our being just average.

But this realization that those who work for and with us are not employees but are **Adults who shape** their own lives —

who know how to lead and manage and to solve problems…

may well be the key to overcoming one of the biggest obstacles to organizational success,

enabling us **to tie in a nearly seamless way** the work we do as managers and with those who work with and for us.

So to wrap up this book:

My colleagues, those who worked with and for me — and the issue of their being ready to take on managing…

are "Adults" — that's who I was working with…

And Watch It Happen Every Day!
_____

And it was "Adults" who were enabling me, as a manager, to get things done not "through" them... but because of them... because they knew how to manage!

As most had not officially held a "management" position in their work lives, and while some may wonder whether people in the group could manage...

again, what I learned and what has stuck in my mind is... knowing they could lead to successfully address and handle operational problems,

and knowing they had to self-manage often to do their jobs well...

and that they had to both lead and manage in their own personal lives...

"I'll Teach You My Job!"

it **began to appear less daunting** to think/envision that they could manage and to take on "The What We Wanted to Look Like."

That is, with each person being able to manage, **not only would we minimize if not** overcome and make up for...

> the adverse impact of the artificial divide that has long been in place between management and those who do the work,

we would also see better working relationships emerge because we are on the same side... working together to bring

And Watch It Happen Every Day!

about important changes that would make for a better organization.

And then this thought formed so clearly in my head...

with more management capacity, we would make more informed and therefore smarter decisions,

we would develop plans and strategies and get better organized to execute the steps to produce the "concrete deliverables" to move the organization forward.

And with that phrase — having more management capacity — sticking in my head,

I overcame my blind spot... realizing that everyone could understand what a manager does and therefore could manage.

But that was not all: Another couple of important BAMS!

If we were able to come to grips with what the person who holds the title of manager (or supervisor or executive) really does every day —

> that is, what I/you thought was important, what we saw work and how we were trying to accomplish things as a manager,

wouldn't knowing that be helpful to
those who worked with and for me?

And Watch It Happen Every Day!
_____

And wouldn't the best way for them to learn would be for me to teach my job?

And if I were able to do this, teaching my job would not only enhance their capacity to "manage" at work, giving us greater management capacity to take on additional projects to better the organization,

teaching my job would prepare them for future professional opportunities.

And as I pondered what I had just written,

I had that second BAM!... that, once again like magic, changed my relationship with those who work with and for me who were "Adults."

"I'll Teach You My Job!"

I can remember so well... actually smiling a bit because it felt right — it just made fabulous sense.

And at our next meeting, I said the following words...

words which I also say to everyone who is a candidate for a job working with and for me.

I know you can lead and I know you can manage,

so, I make the following **commitment to you...**

And Watch It Happen Every Day!

"I hire people who can do my job.

I want to make you who work with and for me so good that others will want to hire you,

**that while it would be great if you stayed with us,
I expect you to leave within a couple of years or perhaps three to five.**

My job is to get you ready!

And to get you ready, I will teach you my job."

"I'll Teach You My Job!"

Book 6 — "You Can't Change People, You Can Only Change the Way You Work with Them"

Those five sentences... **You just read them.**

- I hire people who can do my job.

- I want to make you so good that others will want to hire you.

- While it would be great if you stayed with us, I expect you to leave within a couple of years or perhaps three to five.

- My job is to get you ready!

And Watch It Happen Every Day!
_____

- **And to get you ready, I will teach you my job!**

What was your reaction?

These words certainly are not what any of us have learned to say, been told to say, or expect to hear.

But whether you're a manager, a supervisor. an executive, or an employee, **take a minute and roll them** around in your mind.

If you said them, would you think differently? Do they make you think of doing something in your job differently?

"I'll Teach You My Job!"

And if you said these words to those who worked with and for you,

what impact do you think they would have on them?

I know those words had impact...

because when I said those words to people who worked with and for me or to those who were candidates for jobs,

they all kind of smiled and looked at me with an expression of...

"Did I just hear what I think I just heard?"

And Watch It Happen Every Day!

And while I sensed that they were pondering what these words might mean for their jobs and what future opportunities might open up for them,

I know the biggest impact of these words... is that they changed me.

They changed how I saw my relationship with those who worked with and for me!

And, to explain how those words changed me...

I'm going to go out on a limb and talk

about an experience that I — and probably most parents — have had...

our relationship with our children.

"I'll Teach You My Job!"

As parents, we love our kids, but we've all struggled at times to figure out our children... as they can be somewhat bewildering at times, right?

Why don't they listen to me/us? **Why don't they do** what we tell them to do?

After all, I have very good reasons... all based on a lot of experience!

Yet even though **we think we know better** and we're giving them great advice, we all get the sense that they sometimes don't listen or don't appear to be listening!

So, one day, **I'm talking with a colleague** about getting things across to people at work and also to our kids...

And Watch It Happen Every Day!
_____

and Sandy, who happened to be a social psychologist, listens to me and says,

"Ken, you can't change people. You can only change the way you work with them."

Of course, this goes in one ear and out the other — and **right over my head** as well.

We meet again on another day and she asks how things are going — meaning with my children and the people who work for me.

And as I'm thinking of what to say, **that big glaring light bulb suddenly goes on...**

"I'll Teach You My Job!"

and in that SO crystal-clear moment, the words just came out of my mouth:

"Oh... I don't think we need to talk about that. I think **I just got it!**"

I realized what Sandy had said the first time.

I can't change people, I can only change the way I work with them.

And later, as I thought about those five sentences that I say to everyone who works with and for me,

I realized that those sentences meant that I had changed how I worked with people.

And Watch It Happen Every Day!

That instead of being in the typical managerial role where I was in charge... and expecting them to do what I had directed (like what we mostly expect of our children),

those words meant that, **as we would now have a different relationship...**

I would have to figure out how to change working with those who worked with and for me!

Of course, I felt good about changing our relationship...

however, **as I ran through** my mind what I had committed myself to and how I would work with them...

"I'll Teach You My Job!"

to make them so good that others would want to hire them,

and also that when they would make that decision to leave,

they would be ready because I would teach them my job...

I found myself having a big debate in my head, a debate that you may find yourself having as well if you've rolled those words around in your head.

And what was that debate?

Plain and simple, like every other manager I've known, **I realized that I didn't have any**

And Watch It Happen Every Day!

real commitment to those who worked with and for me!

Repeat:

I, just like probably every other manager who sees him/herself as being in charge,

just never thought that it was important to have a commitment to those who worked with and for me!

That thought simply never occurred to me. It never crossed my mind. But **when I realized this harsh reality**... I was frankly disappointed in myself...

and right then and there, I knew that I needed to do something.

So, first, I had an understandable thought... because of what we had accomplished and that I really liked those who worked with and for me... and I think most of them liked me,

my primary sense was that I, like any boss, was very grateful to them for all they had done... and that they were pleased as well.

But given that we had to take on even more — the "What We Wanted to Look Like," being grateful because of what they had done in helping achieve superb success...

It just felt inadequate... that gratitude could contribute nothing to making us better... that it didn't provide a path forward.

And Watch It Happen Every Day!

But then those five sentences came into my head and changed everything!

Why? Because those five sentences meant that... rather than being grateful — a nice sentiment, but which was backward-looking,

this commitment I had made to each person to teach him/her my job...

had created the basis for new, proactive, forward-looking, mutually beneficial relationship!

I can't over-emphasize the impact that making a commitment had on me.

That is, once I understood that that the people who worked with and for me were "Adults," I could no longer rely on the employer-employee relationship.

And I got two powerful insights with a different twist... about concepts that are familiar to those of us who are managers.

The first was the concept – "almost a rule" that we've all heard, but now I came to see in a very different and helpful way that impacted directly how I would work with those who reported to me.

And Watch It Happen Every Day!

___

And what was that concept?

"It All Starts with the Boss."

The second insight was about a concept that most managers haven't heard/are probably not familiar with...

And the reason we haven't heard of it is, as there is an implied criticism in the concept **which questions our ability to manage —**

the decisions we make and, most importantly, whether the decisions we make are the right/best decisions,

it just isn't something we're usually taught or have learned and/or frankly may not want to hear.

"I'll Teach You My Job!"

This was a concept that I had heard a number of years ago, but at the time didn't really understand the importance of it when working with people.

"If you are going to affect someone but you don't include them,

the only role you leave them is the role of the critic."

As this second concept is something few of us have heard, read it again because it has significant implications for our work as managers...

And once you've read it, set it aside... as we'll discuss this concept later in this book.

And Watch It Happen Every Day!
___

Let's back up and talk about…

"It all starts with the boss."

Typically, those of us who are in charge take this to mean, **"We call the shots."**

As much as this concept is just a widely understood assumption about managing, in my case, however, **even though I was "in charge"** and had the responsibilities to call the shots… determining strategy, direction, goals, and the work to be undertaken,

more than a few of my efforts —

experiences that others may have also had in their organizations or businesses —

"I'll Teach You My Job!"

even though I had spent many days and weeks putting together the strategy or a program,

didn't succeed as I would like... and ended up not being implemented as envisioned or were set aside.

But after I had made that commitment to teach my job, **I had another of those "AHA" moments...**

and I saw in a very different way what "It All Starts with the Boss" meant.

I thought back to what I said in Book 3 — "Coming to Grips with Managing." I know I struggled as a manager, but even though I needed help,

And Watch It Happen Every Day!

because what I had read about managing and/or had "learned" from observing and talking with others…

didn't lead to astounding success/didn't work,

I realized that, if I were to get better as a manager, "It All Starts with the Boss" was not about "calling the shots,"

what it meant was that it was up to me; that is, if I were to get better, **it was simply up to me** to overcome the shortcomings that limited me as a manager.

It was up to me to take the initiative and come up with ways that would enable me to work more effectively with those who worked with and for me.

"I'll Teach You My Job!"

And this made great sense... because, even though I had made that commitment —

given the simple reality of the dynamics in the workplace, while I had great people working with and for me,

I knew that they were not going to speak up in a meeting and say that I should therefore teach them my job.

So, I had the initial excitement that came from realizing that both changing my job and teaching it was up to me, but then I had a more important second **"AHA!"** moment related to teaching my job...

Even though I strongly felt that learning my job...

And Watch It Happen Every Day!

would help them to do their jobs well.

and would also likely lead to changes in their careers... and that it was up to me to take the initiative,

I saw that there was an even **greater benefit that would likely not happen any other way.**

That, by my taking the initiative to teach my job so that people learned what I would do as a manager and strengthen their capacity to manage in the context of the work we were doing,

what would happen – what would only happen because it started with me as the boss taking that initiative was that **we would create more management capacity.**

And by creating more management capacity **we would overcome the shortcomings that I had as a single person in charge…**

> where we've all been taught to rely upon a single person to lead and to manage…

and thus **be better able to take on** these projects and initiatives — "The What We Wanted to Look Like" — where managing well would be essential.

After realizing we could have more management capacity, I had the second conceptual breakthrough I mentioned above that would strengthen how I/we managed.

And Watch It Happen Every Day!

The background was our organization faced the real possibility of a collective bargaining election... and a management consultant had been brought to talk about why people move toward unionization.

This consultant said two things:

"People can live with bad decisions, what they can't accept is bad decision making."

To which he added:

"If you're going to affect someone and you don't include them,

the only role you leave them is the role of the critic."

And he then went on to explain the implications of what he had said.

He said that **when an executive** (or a manager or a supervisor) makes a decision without input or doesn't seek that input, that way of making a decision isn't acceptable.

And the reason it's not acceptable is the second sentence… That, as any **decision will affect** some, if not a number of people, and if they don't like the decision,

and didn't have input or were caught unaware by the decision and were adversely affected, because they know that they have been disregarded,

And Watch It Happen Every Day!

the only thing **they can do is to criticize** the decision.

Thus, by excluding those who are affected...

not just employees but also some managers and directors and supervisors as well as when needed the views/interests of clients and customers,

when we, as those in charge, act as if we alone had the capacity to make decisions and that the decisions that we make are the best decisions,

and those decisions don't work or have adverse impact,

the consequence is that we... **leave them with**

the only role they can play which is "the role of the critic."

That people will "second-guess" and readily express their dissatisfaction and/or be critical —

> whether openly or by being passive-aggressive... or, as we also know, making the decision to leave.

should come as no surprise... we've all seen it happen and have experienced it.

Understanding that a bad process of decision making can create distrustful relationships... if not a nearly **insurmountable rift** between leadership and those who work, supervise, and/or manage...

And Watch It Happen Every Day!

as well as even perhaps with those who have higher level management responsibilities – who may even report to you if "you're in charge."

Whereas, involving those who might be affected would create better relationships if not a stronger bond,

I realized that by making that commitment to teach them my job...

people would see that — by learning my job, they would now have a new role. And, in taking on that role where they would now provide directly critical input in decision-making,

they would also know that their involvement may well lead to better decisions affecting the work they do and also have impact on the organization.

In closing this book, I know that what I've written isn't what most of us have read in management books... or have learned in classes or at work.

You won't find what I discussed in this Book 6... **a discussion about the person in charge making a commitment** to those who work with and for you to teach his/her job.

You won't find a discussion about...

- I can't change people... that I can only change the way I work with them;

- the importance of rethinking "It all starts with the boss" ... that teaching my job would only happen if I took the initiative to make that commitment to do that;

    or

And Watch It Happen Every Day!

- the insight about the adverse impact of how we make decisions which would often leave people with the role of critic.

And if we tie what I just wrote in this Book 6 to people who come to work with the capacity to lead and manage because they are "shaping their own lives."

that those who work with and for us are "Adults" and not employees,

this commitment to teach my job — by changing how I worked with people which leads to building more management capacity

is what will lead to greater success and accomplishment!

"I'll Teach You My Job!"

Let's now turn to the next books where these ideas found expression in what I did.

And Watch It Happen Every Day!

Book 7 — The Book Specifically for Those of Us "Who Are in Charge"

Read the following as an introduction to this book.

We know that we **don't have easy jobs**. We know that burnout is high, that interruptions occur on many days. Yet we're expected to still get things done.

A few of us fortunately have some pretty strong people working with and for us who just always **seem to come through; people we can count on to get the job done!**

However, for most of us, as managers, supervisors or executives, we know that in the face of breakdowns (motors, equipment, supply shortages, lost documents), unexpected changes in priorities and rushed deadlines, we have to be ready to intervene... to roll up our sleeves and do whatever is needed to get things done.

And again, for most of us, we've been able to get the job done — and sometimes to even excel. However, **having experienced** frequent crises and been victimized by poor processes as well as gaps in skills and knowledge (even *though people were well-intended and motivated) over a number of years, I came to understand that, as long as we continued to work this way — to react and then to intervene, that as long as we continued to play this management version of **"Whack a Mole,"** we would never raise our effectiveness to a new level because fundamentally things never just quite work as they should.*

If what has just been described somewhat fits your situation, you may well find this book to be helpful.

So, **let's bring this home** to all of us who are managers.

At the beginning of the previous book, I asked you to think about the impact of the five sentences on those who worked with and for you.

And Watch It Happen Every Day!

Now let's go one step further... and add a little twist.

If you took these five sentences **to your boss** and gave them to him/her...what would s/he say?

How do you think your boss would react... do you think he/she would change?

And further, **if your boss had said** those words to you, how would you react?

Obviously, the words in these five sentences are different...

I know I never heard them said by anyone I had worked for.

"I'll Teach You My Job!"

And in talking with numerous other people, they also hadn't heard any boss they had worked for say words like these.

As these words are powerful,

I'm going to talk about how those words resulted in changing how I worked with people, impacting our relationship, and enabling us to become amazingly effective!

So, Let's Look at Those Five Sentences:

As the first sentence...

And Watch It Happen Every Day!

"I hire people who can do my job"

clearly goes against conventional wisdom —

>the standard practice of hiring at entry level or in a position with clearly defined duties and responsibilities,

the obvious question is...

what is the value of hiring someone —

>whether a professional, a technician,
>
>an expert in finance or technology,
>
>a maintenance worker,
>
>a support staff member,
>
>an assembly-line worker,

"I'll Teach You My Job!"

or someone in sales or distribution...

who can do my job?

I'm going to come at this indirectly, but I think anyone who is a manager or a supervisor **would recognize** the following.

As I was gathering information for this book, I had a discussion with a manager about how his company — a technology firm — evaluated people.

He said that they used **two dimensions: performance and potential.**

And Watch It Happen Every Day!

And since technology is essentially bimodal, this made sense.

You measure performance simply by looking at whether people can do the jobs that they were hired to do.

> Do you know enough to quickly write effective programming code?

Straight forward... It's a one or a zero
— 1/0... yes/no.

Either you can or you can't. If you can't, the program won't execute.

As painful as it may be for some of us, remember our days of studying math?

"I'll Teach You My Job!"

You either knew math and got the right answer or you didn't know math and you either couldn't complete the problem or you got the wrong answer.

Now I know many will not agree with me, but using tech and math as analogies, I got this sudden insight...

Performance is not multi-level, it's bimodal.

You either succeed in doing the job or you fall short.

So, bear with me in the following discussion.

And Watch It Happen Every Day!

As many of you know, this bi-modal approach goes against what we've all been taught and used for years...

that set of multi-level evaluation criteria (e.g., outstanding, above average, acceptable, needs improvement, unacceptable).

And while this multi-level approach to performance management is not effective —

is there really anyone who would say it is?

it's the approach most of us use.

However, it wasn't my intention to talk about whether to use bimodal or multi-level evaluation performance criteria... or to debate the rationale for either.

I was writing about performance as **the gateway** to a discussion about potential.

What we know is that potential is different from performance, and the important question with respect to potential is...

potential for what?

Whether it's in technology, the services industry, healthcare, finance, or manufacturing... it doesn't matter the business, the easy answer on potential is...

And Watch It Happen Every Day!

---

higher level responsibility/more complex work requiring more technical or professional expertise.

The problem, however, with seeing potential this way is that, as there's only so far one can go as an individual with greater technical/professional responsibilities —

and this is where the thinking gets a little slippery...
when we talk about potential,

what we're really talking about is doing a job beyond mastery of the skills and knowledge at the highest level needed for work related to our current job.

That is,

regardless of unique organizational realities and their implications — matrix organizations, hierarchical/top-down, command and control or the kind of business...

as projects get more complex, and more and more people of necessity must be involved,

what is absolutely essential... is the ability to work with people,

particularly, the ability to have them work collaboratively if the project is to be successful.

Thus, the real manifestation of potential is not as an expert... **but is realized in the ability to**

And Watch It Happen Every Day!

work with people to enhance the likelihood of success!

And, to cut to the chase and drive home the point for all of us who are managers,

when we talk about working with people in order to achieve success, **aren't we really talking about supervising and managing and leading?**

And, if that is the case, when we're hiring someone, we should not just focus on whether someone can do the job... or whether they may be able to attain technical mastery.

What we should be looking at...

is their potential from the perspective that potential is really about supervising people or managing programs and people.

If this perspective with respect to potential makes sense,

what better place to start than to have that in mind from the beginning…

that is, "hire people who can do your job" when you are choosing to bring someone on board.

Let's turn to the second sentence…

"I want to make you so good that others will want to hire you"

And Watch It Happen Every Day!
_____

Making someone so good others will want to hire them follows logically from considering potential in the first place when hiring people.

As we all know, businesses and organizations have chosen so-called "high-potential" individuals to prepare them to move up when an opportunity/a promotion presents itself.

These individuals receive special treatment —

> coaching, mentoring, special assignments, and priority in succession planning —

to acquire the skills and knowledge to prepare them to step in when a vacancy occurs or a new position becomes available.

"I'll Teach You My Job!"

However, **we know that these efforts have had, at best, mixed results...**

What we know is that, more often than not, there is no one who is ready —

> people are promoted prematurely and can't do the job...

> especially when a vacancy unexpectedly occurs and the position must be filled quickly...

and thus we find it still necessary to run external searches to bring in talent from "outside"

Or, in the worst case of all,

And Watch It Happen Every Day!

the "high-potentials" whom we have groomed... and made considerable investments in, instead of waiting,

have already left, taking positions elsewhere.

And why have these approaches to prepare people to move up in an organization failed?

My view is that they all have **the same fatal flaw...**

"I'll Teach You My Job!"

an assumption that focusing on a person or a small select group of individuals — those with "high potential" — is what a smart organization or business should do.

> After all, as there are only so many resources (time and money), shouldn't we focus on those who are most likely to move up?

However, as I said, this approach has had results that consistently fall short.

In contrast, teaching our jobs as managers, supervisors, or executives to all who work with and for you or me...

not only actualizes the "potential" which everyone has,

teaching our jobs to everyone who works with and for us also means — importantly for the organization,

And Watch It Happen Every Day!

___

that there will always be someone ready to step up and step in...

because they know our jobs whether we're a manager, a supervisor, or an executive!

And what boss or organization wouldn't want that?

This job of making people so good that others will want to hire them is all up to the leader...

"It all starts with the boss!"

and for us as leaders to make this happen, we will be doing different work with a different mindset... which, again, is to teach everyone our jobs and do so as part of our daily work!

"I'll Teach You My Job!"

Let's now turn to the third sentence.

"While it would be great if you stayed with us, I expect you to leave within a couple of years or perhaps three to five."

Obviously, this third sentence follows from the first two sentences.

It's inevitable that at some time people who have learned my/your job are going to leave.

When I had this sentence come into my head, it was inspiring and powerful…

And Watch It Happen Every Day!

I simply liked it; but **isn't it also illogical?**

After all, doesn't this sentence openly encourage people who have strong talents, who are highly effective, who know our jobs... to leave?

Of course, the sentence can be interpreted as doing that.

But what the sentence did for me... was that it enabled me **to convey a positive, very supportive message...**

an acknowledgement to those who worked with and for me that I recognized they not only had the potential, but **had also experienced the actual achievement** of becoming so good... that someday they would make the decision to leave and go to work elsewhere.

Thus, for me, this sentence conveyed something that we all want but too often don't get... that I had great confidence in them!

I wanted them to know — with their capacity to lead and manage and the work they were doing —

that they were ready...

and that I knew they could manage and lead and would achieve great success!

And Watch It Happen Every Day!

And while a few did leave for new, more significant jobs, **most stayed on** (other than those who were egregiously bad whom I had encouraged to leave)!

And the fourth and fifth sentences?

"My job is to get you ready!"

"And to get you ready, I will teach you my job!"

When did things just click with Ellen, Patrice, Dalena, Dan, Gary, Francesca, Landy, Lohan, and Erik in our group?

"I'll Teach You My Job!"

I think **things kicked in...** when those five sentences helped me get my head in the right place...

and I made that commitment to teach my job.

So how did I get them ready?

If I were going to live by what I just wrote, what was more important?

Having more brains — meaning more informed minds working on issues and problems versus the "downside" issue...

of fearing that somehow they were going to be intruding on what I was to be doing as the manager?

And Watch It Happen Every Day!
───────────────────────────────────

Hardly a choice at all...

I needed the best of their thinking and insight to put together... the best in programming and services and those concrete deliverables!

And that certainly wasn't going to happen by standing in front of them and give a presentation to tell them this is my job.

Here's an experience of one of the people who worked for me.

Patrice wrote:

"You encouraged us to think of the best way to do something...You would tell us that, because we run our own lives and households, we were capable of doing it

"I'll Teach You My Job!"

here... We all exhibited self-confidence and were willing to try anything."

For example, I remember when you gave me a camera and asked me to go out and shoot pictures to include in our new employee orientation program.

(We had a terrible orientation program...)

I had never done such a thing — but you were so encouraging and supportive. So, I learned how to use that camera and went out and shot those pictures, and how to build them into the orientation program!

And this great collage of photos that Patrice put together that introduction – that welcoming introduction conveying a sense of belonging, of being a part of where we all worked.

Notably, Patrice not only stepped up and managed this special project, as she was also the key person who managed the calendar for our group, she demonstrated that she had the capacity to lead and to manage!

And Watch It Happen Every Day!

And thus, it was easy to make the decision that the best way to get people ready was "to teach them my job!"

Did teaching my job work? Was this effective?

While I will talk in greater detail about teaching my job in Book 9,

as one of the biggest outcomes was to draw forth the best in thinking and problem-solving and to actualize their capacity to lead and to manage —

and to avoid putting people in the role of the critic,

I want to share the following example that makes this point:

"I'll Teach You My Job!"

Did you notice that in the book are ideas or comments from or about people who worked with and for me?

I didn't come up with that. It came about because Dalena read an early draft of what I had written... and said in her usual "up-front" and direct way,

"Well, that's all about you, Ken. What about us? **Why isn't what we would say or do in your book?"**

Dalena was doing what had become our practice in how we handled our operational problems, the issues of culture and the development and implementation of concrete deliverables.

And Watch It Happen Every Day!

She was pointing out that, when it came to this book, **I had "fallen short!"**

She was saying, "Doesn't our input matter?" which, of course, it did. It was critical to making a difference —to make the best decisions.

But I had just missed it as I began writing this book. I was looking for positive feedback on early drafts when I met with Dalena, and...

while **it was a bit hard** to take,

she gave me something better... that I needed to hear.

Because she didn't pull any punches and said what she saw as a big mistake — a monumental oversight!

"I'll Teach You My Job!"

And I'm grateful to Dalena — as I've been on many occasions throughout our relationship over the years.

So, to get the thoughts and ideas of those who worked with and for me into this book meant that I had to **involve them** in putting this book together.

Over the months, I've reached out to each person and asked for their thoughts and comments... and to get feedback.

Not only did I change the content of this book,

I've gone even further, also getting comments from others who didn't work with or for me....

>managers, directors, supervisors, employees as well as executives

And Watch It Happen Every Day!

And there is no question the book is so much richer for what they said.

Because Dalena's comments brought home the biggest point...

 involving everyone and getting their best thoughts and experiences...

is the key — **essential not only to running an operation or an organization...**

but also to writing a book — a better book!

But because if I didn't involve them, her criticism made it clear that...

> "the only role I was leaving them was the role of the critic."

SOME THOUGHTS TO PONDER:

If there's such an upside for us who are managers, supervisors, or executives to work with these five sentences in mind,

why isn't it done?

We know a lot of the reasons:

The mindset of "being in charge"...

And Watch It Happen Every Day!

---

the strong presence/influence of long-standing organizational lore that divides responsibilities into leading and managing from executing... the work people are doing in their daily activities.

I also know what I've said previously...

that, as it all begins with the boss... if the person in charge — the boss to whom you report doesn't see it,

these desirable changes likely won't occur.

However, even under those circumstances I just described, I've come to realize that **we've not run into a wall.**

"I'll Teach You My Job!"

So, just as we all do in our own lives and with our own work where you and I have the capacity to lead and to manage,

you and I can take the initiative when it comes to the challenge of getting your boss to teach you his/her job.

And while you might be reluctant to do this, here's what I would like you to think about...

A thought in line with what we discussed in Book 6,

"You can't change people, you can only change the way you work with them!"

Think of it this way...

And Watch It Happen Every Day!
_____

How would you react if someone asked you to teach your job to him/her?

I know it would give me pause at first... However, I believe we all understand if you want to learn your boss' job...

but expect your boss to take the initiative to do so, it's not likely to happen.

So, as you know what you want, **use a direct approach** and simply go and ask your boss to teach his/her job!

Now, you might think that's pretty bold... but guess what, you just might get a positive reception!

"I'll Teach You My Job!"

and, if I were the boss, I might be a bit intrigued about doing it!

I believe most bosses — especially those who have been around a while and have had somewhat and maybe even quite productive careers, would actually be flattered if you asked them!

While this may seem daunting at first — asking your boss to teach you his/her job is something you already know how to do.

It really is just the same as taking on other concrete deliverables. In this case, what you want is... by the end of xxx period, to know your boss' job,

And because you're the one taking the initiative to make this particular concrete deliverable happen, **isn't**

And Watch It Happen Every Day!

your stepping forward to do this really a terrific demonstration of your capacity to lead and to manage...

where you can make the changes that will enhance your impact and effectiveness by taking actions to bring about desired charge — in this case learning your boss' job!

And once again, I **didn't come up** with this. In talking with a television associate producer, Jillian said exactly that.

When I asked how she would approach a boss who might be somewhat reluctant to teach you his/her job, she smiled and said,

"I would say, **'I really admire you!'"** Now, how can anyone resist that?

"I'll Teach You My Job!"

Think about it! Relationships are not about logic — they're not about being hierarchical, they're emotional! And If you make the emotional connection — which I believe this kind of statement will do,

there is no question that **your boss will have that emotional connection...** and be invested in you... seeing you in a new way because s/he will realize that you may well be carrying their legacy, giving a longer life to their work, their thinking, and their influence and impact...

and what boss wouldn't like that!

NOTE: If you're feeling somewhat reluctant, you might simply give your boss this book and set up some times when the two of you can meet to talk about the ideas and practices found in "Ill Teach You My Job!"

And Watch It Happen Every Day!

Addendum to Book 7 — The Book for Those of Us in Charge

The example of "Dave" who didn't know the jobs of his bosses.

*One of the best financial people I ever worked with was "Dave" (not his real name). Dave was simply sharp with a **bear trap of a mind** for detail which is exactly what you want in the person in charge of the budget.*

*However, one of **the big irritants** about Dave was that he thought his colleagues in other offices were lazy.*

He would openly say things like:

"They don't come in to work at 8 like the rest of us...They come in whenever they want. We're in our offices and there are still at home. Sometimes they even say they're working at home... they're sitting on their patios!"

Even though these were great research and development people who often worked in the evenings and during the weekends whereas the rest of us were doing our 40-hour workweek and not putting in weekend hours, on nearly

"I'll Teach You My Job!"

every occasion when he had an opportunity, Dave always recommended cutting back on this group even though they were "core" — the critical group in the organization.

*What if Dave **had known the job of the CEO** to whom he reported? What s/he was trying to accomplish, would Dave be recommending cutting this group?*

*If he knew the division head's job, would he recommend cutting this group? If he had **greater appreciation** and knowledge of the strategic plan or priorities, would he have had realized that, even in the face of cuts, things don't grind to a halt, that we have to keep going and in fact get better which is what these people were doing.*

However, Dave leaned on the issue of office hours to justify his view that cutting this group was what had to be done.

If Dave had had the opportunity to learn the jobs of others, rather than being adversarial/contentious and an irritant, I think he could have had a positive impact that definitely would have put him more in sync.

Word got out about** Dave's views and, even though he was a key figure, he found himself **faced with a limited

And Watch It Happen Every Day!

upside... kept somewhat on the sidelines. He had great skills, and even though he was the logical choice to become the vice-president for finance, but he never received serious consideration.

I told this story about Dave to **make a couple** *of points:*

There are costs **when we are narrowly** *circumscribed because long-standing organizational practices lock us in as to what we regard as our jobs. We have the belief that we're actually organized the best way, but given the example of Dave,* **isn't there the possibility** *that there are ways to be better organized? Dave was adversely affected, but I think also hurt the organization and what the leaders were trying to accomplish.*

That Dave and others who saw their jobs narrowly isn't necessarily their fault. Dave's not going to tell his boss to teach him (Dave or any of us who report to someone) his/her job.

If leadership in crucial to organizational success, then isn't part of leadership teaching people our jobs, making people so good that they are highly effective colleagues who work with us toward ends we share – who not only do a superb job in the work they do, but **are so good because they know our jobs that others would want to hire them***?*

"I'll Teach You My Job!"

Book 8 — The Twice-Weekly Meetings... Some Hold Them Every Day or Twice-a-Day

Before I get to the "nitty-gritty" of how I changed working with people and how I taught people my job,

there is first a **piece of business** that needs to be covered.

In the introductory Book 1, I mentioned the twice-weekly meetings. The importance of these meetings can't be overlooked.

These meetings were where everything came together:

And Watch It Happen Every Day!

When I showed a draft of this book to a colleague who was the officer just below the president in her organization — someone I hadn't seen for a number of years, she gave me a "knowing smile" and said that in her group, the people who reported to her, they met not just twice-weekly, but every day — five days a week, first thing in the morning to hear what others were working on, to share information, and to get everyone on the same page.

Operational activities and processes, workplace challenges with egregiously bad individuals, concrete deliverables — "The What We Wanted to Look Like,"

and leveraging our individual and collective capacity to manage and lead.

These meetings kept us on track... they **helped inform everyone** about the specifics of what each of us was working on.

"I'll Teach You My Job!"

And by informing everyone what each of us was doing,

and especially after we flattened the organization...

essentially creating the same/complementary jobs for everyone which led to people working collaboratively to solve problems,

we came to **really know each other's jobs.**

But the best part of these meetings is that they got everyone on the same page.

We all see the same daily schedule...

And Watch It Happen Every Day!
_____

what are we working on today and what will we be working on tomorrow,

the calendar of upcoming events, the activities to accomplish, what has to be done by which deadlines,

and we also keep in front of everyone the concrete deliverables of "What We Want to Look Like."

The meetings are also a time when **new issues or challenges that have just emerged** can be brought to the attention of everyone…

and the **synergy of their experiences and insights brought to bear to develop solutions.**

"I'll Teach You My Job!"

In addition,

as the twice-weekly meetings **provided the opportunity for everyone** to use their leadership and management capacities to bring about/further their own success as well as that of the group,

these meetings reinforced their confidence that what they are doing…

and that how they are leading and managing is having **a positive impact** in making us more productive and effective.

And, finally, these meetings are also a time when people **can learn what I do…**

And Watch It Happen Every Day!
_____

not as a lecture or presentation but **in the course of doing our daily work.**

Lohan said: I "hated" these twice-weekly meetings at that time, but "what was great every day we could share information, and not just listen to the boss."

"Every day we spend some time and he come back from vacation and has new ideas and talks about whatever in these meetings. But it worked, we all got the same information, we understood."

Ken's comment: In retrospect, while it was appropriate that we were focused on our operational work and the concrete deliverables as well as newly-emerged challenges and problems, these twice-weekly meetings expanded to include a quick review of office infrastructure and logistics which if not working properly could impede our work.

Was anybody having problems with their computer? Were the printers in working order? Any supplies needed? Anything broken? Could you not find something readily? Has anyone seen this file, a form from..., a document? What wasn't organized? Was something missing? What about the website? Our client interface?

We should be asking, what do we need do to minimize/eliminate obstacles that keep us from doing our work so that we can be highly effective!

ARE THESE TWICE-WEEKLY MEETINGS REALLY THAT DIFFERENT?

Since everybody already holds staff meetings, questions have been raised about these twice-weekly meetings and their value.

- "Isn't having a twice-weekly standing meeting just a more frequent variation of staff meetings that

And Watch It Happen Every Day!
_____

are held on a weekly, bi-weekly, or monthly basis?"

- "Meeting more frequently seems to take up a lot of time. Isn't it more valuable that people just use that time do their jobs?"

- "Help us understand the benefits of these meetings so I can weigh the trade-off."

Holding standing meetings is not *unusual. Most organizations and businesses already hold such meetings on a regular, if not daily, basis.*

For example, supervisors and managers in facilities hold standing meetings with work crews before the day's activities begin to get organized/go over the day's work and for the manager/supervisor to share information.

"I'll Teach You My Job!"

Or teachers, broken out by their respective teaching areas or grade levels – meet with the teacher who is serving as the chair of their group. Those meetings may occur bi-weekly or monthly with an agenda developed by the chair/department head.

While these kinds of meetings have been SOP, having meetings with this structure where the manager or supervisor is in charge – running the meeting, is a missed opportunity.

In the usual standing meeting, the leader sets the agenda and the meeting is led by that individual. The leader provides information that s/he thinks needs to be shared. But the problem is that, as meetings organized this way only provide a sporadic opportunity for employees to provide feedback, the leader misses the opportunity to learn what's not working/what needs to be improved.

While employees may in advance submit their ideas/responses to the proposed agenda or at the meeting ask questions or make a comment or two, as employee/attendee input is almost always sought at the end of the meeting, these meetings by the way they're structured and led send a clear message:

Employees have no real active role; they really shouldn't

And Watch It Happen Every Day!

be raising issues. Rather they should listen to what they're told and then go about their daily tasks.

However, if each employee is provided the leadership opportunity to lead these meetings, all of them will be able to discuss matters that might otherwise not be raised. But, so long as leaders think they should run these meetings, while they may provide a few minutes at the end of the meeting where employees may raise questions/issues, employees don't see this as a serious effort to find out what they have on their minds. And, since leaders aren't mind readers who know what's on employees' minds/what they are thinking, they remain out of touch with employees and the issues that are important to them.

Invariably I also got this comment:

"Since employees-as-managers are taking on managerial responsibilities, how can we assure managers or

"I'll Teach You My Job!"

supervisors that **these meetings should not be taken as a threat** to them?"

Being sensitive to the fact that some managers may question giving up two key responsibilities —

> leading the group as well as the setting the agenda...

the following **can't be emphasized enough.**

The leadership opportunity is **not meant to or designed** to replace anyone who officially holds the management responsibility.

The manager is always the person with the organizational responsibility for the work done and the effectiveness of the group.

And Watch It Happen Every Day!

We might think the rationale is implicitly clear for the manager to have these organizational responsibilities for the work done and the group's productivity. However, in Book 9, what a manager, supervisor, or executive explicitly does on a daily basis that contributes directly to the daily work of those who work with and for him/her is described with a set of clear activities.

Those who are managers should also note that, because of the way these meetings are organized with a very clear and known agenda for each meeting —

these meetings readily facilitate **what any manager** would want:

"I'll Teach You My Job!"

___

1. What are we **scheduled to handle** that day?

2. What didn't we complete from yesterday?

3. What are we going to be working on tomorrow?

4. What should we be aware of that will be **coming up** on the calendar?

5. What deadlines are we facing?

6. Where are we on putting together/implementing the concrete deliverables?

7. And what **other items** — anything unexpected as well as information from the manager — are important to share with everyone?

In addition to assuring that work is getting taken care of, one of the best things about these meetings…

And Watch It Happen Every Day!

is that they create benefits that would not occur other than through these employee-as-leader meetings.

As we know, these are adults who are quite effective at leading their own lives and solving problems as well as prioritizing and making decisions outside of the workplace.

What these meetings enable is for those same individuals as employees-as-leaders **to bring those talents** and knowledge and experiences — all deriving from their capacities to lead and to manage —

to our organizations and businesses to improve our work.

"I'll Teach You My Job!"

These meetings through employees in the role as leaders also free individuals —

who in their previous relationships of "being supervised" might have held back and deferred —

to be **more forthcoming...**

      to share information and perspectives that are often critical to not only getting our daily work done, but also to solving problems, resolving challenges in the workplace, and making the best decisions.

Finally, **keep in mind that** with numerous managers being regarded as less than successful leaders —

And Watch It Happen Every Day!

again, through no fault of their own because they are working in a management system with built-in flaws,

these meetings, by providing the leadership opportunity which develops and engages more management capacity...

compensate for that major shortcoming of current management practices —

the limitations of the single manager-as-leader, "I'm in charge!" approach.

And, best of all, by taking on management responsibilities as "employees-as-leaders" where they **call on their capacities** to lead and to manage, these meetings enable people to not only learn what I do in my job as a manager…

they also provide those each individual with the opportunity to demonstrate in actual practice on a daily basis…

that they know how to manage effectively because they are taking the lead to resolve important matters…

just as the manager, supervisor, or executive would be doing.

So, let's turn to the dynamics of these twice-weekly meetings.

And Watch It Happen Every Day!

HOW ARE THE TWICE-WEEKLY MEETINGS ORGANIZED?

There are **two key activities** that make these meetings effective:

- A clear process to choose the leader.
- How the meeting is run.

Again, because these meetings are different, what is the value of organizing these meetings around these two activities?

Is it really worth the hassle of having to decide who runs each meeting just so that each employee can have the leadership opportunity?

"I'll Teach You My Job!"

Ellen noted: I thought the standing meetings were productive. People had to be accountable on a daily basis! We weren't dragged to those meetings, we found them useful.

I asked Martha, "What are you working on?"

And when she'd reply with something like, "I'm working on some issues."

I'd ask, "What issues? Don't need names, but we're here to share; to tell what's going on so we can keep on top of stuff and help each other out!"

Yolanda said: Pam was in charge of the calendar, and she was not shy and would talk about what had to be done and who was to do it!

It is important to note that not everyone who worked with me agreed with these twice-weekly meetings.

When I talked with Gilbert, he said: I didn't like these meetings. I had a lot of things to do and here we are talking about what each other is doing.

And Watch It Happen Every Day!

Ken's comment – For years, we have talked about organizational silos, trying to overcome the isolation these silos create. But so long as people do not share/want to share information, these silos will continue to exist, inhibiting communication that people need to do their jobs with an adverse impact on our overall effectiveness.

It's completely understandable that people want to work on that which they can control. If we focus on our work, then the success of the work we do is up to each of us. But since the work of each is really only a part of a greater process, it is important to change the mindset where each person's focus is only on what each she/he has to do.

If you are in a group, whatever your role or responsibilities, you have to realize that what may be going on — what's working/not working, what may be occurring that's causing a problem or issue, or what other people are doing — can have direct impact on whether you make a mistake or you are able to do your work quickly and accurately and/or are able to solve a problem.

"I'll Teach You My Job!"

Also isn't having different people in the leader role really just going to **be confusing and possibly chaotic** since no two people will run these meetings in the same way?

Why not just choose someone and hold the meeting?

The sentiment to **just select a leader** and get on with the meeting is understandable.

But there are benefits to choosing the leader in a certain way.

When we started out, I decided to **choose the leader alphabetically**; that is, by first name and this individual is the leader for three meetings at a minimum and sometimes for four or five meetings.

And Watch It Happen Every Day!

This again wasn't by any design,

but what I found, by selecting the leader this way, is that **there were just amazing benefits** that built each person's capacity to lead and manage within our group.

As we know, because people may not have had formal management responsibility previously, they may understandably be reluctant to lead —

and being uncertain of their own skills and knowledge, **they may want to avoid** being the leader.

However, in the twice-weekly meeting format,

with each person knowing s/he will be the leader and approximately when s/he will assume that responsibility and for how long,

that individual came to look at these meetings differently.

They realized, when they are in the role of employee-as-leader,

that they have a major responsibility...

of assuring the **seamless continuity** of the group's work that may have begun under a different individual.

And in order to effectively lead the meeting,

And Watch It Happen Every Day!

they not only can't tune out or only partially listen (reading their email, etc.) during these meetings when someone else is "the leader" of the meeting,

they also realized,

> because for any meeting the person who is supposed to be leading the meeting

may be absent that day (other pressing matters – business-related or personal),

that he/she or any other person **is expected to step forward and lead the meeting.**

And knowing that he/she may/will have to pick up and continue the discussions and decision-making had a surprising impact...

they saw their presence in these meetings in a different way.

They understood the importance of participating fully in the discussions — that it's essential to keep on top of the topics/issues…

so that they are ready to step in whenever needed —

and be the leader who is prepared to manage the meetings **which is what a manager has to do!**

And Watch It Happen Every Day!

That this will be challenging at first to many in the employee-as-leader role is understandable...

as the daily schedule and ongoing calendar and the issues and concerns tied to the "What We Want to Look Like" **may lie outside** of their job responsibilities and expertise.

But since all of these —

as well as problems that **arise unexpectedly** for which there aren't ready answers —

are precisely what managers face every day,

what the employee-as-leader will experience by utilizing their capacities to lead and to manage...

"I'll Teach You My Job!"

is a vast expansion of their knowledge…

a broadening of their awareness of the work and thinking of others in the group as well as the manager's perspective beyond their immediate jobs…

and in leading and managing these twice-weekly meetings, as they learn what I and any other manager has to do…

they will learn my job… and be on the path to becoming "so good others will want to hire them!"

And Watch It Happen Every Day!

What follows is a description of how we focused our time and energy during these twice-weekly meetings.

A: For the Review of the Daily Schedule — spend 10-15 minutes

Everyone is expected to have reviewed the calendar prior to the meeting and to be "up-to-speed" on what has to be done.

We asked if we are taking care of the items on the daily schedule...

and are we prepared for the upcoming items on the calendar?

And we also asked...

what each of us is doing today, hadn't completed from the previous day, and what we need to take of tomorrow — as well as the deadlines.

B: For the Concrete Deliverables — "The What We Want to Look Like" — spend 15 minutes

we focused on updates and asked for status reports on the various initiatives.

Again, knowing that everything can't be completed for a variety of reasons... that **unexpected issues** or problems have arisen,

And Watch It Happen Every Day!
___

we either discussed/resolved how to best proceed...

scheduling that item for the next meeting or **developing/putting in place a quick work plan** to get the matter taken care of in subsequent meetings.

(Note: We found it best to focus on one concrete deliverable at any one time.

However, there may be occasions where two may be undertaken, but that may stretch people's time and other resources as well as lead to loss of focus and timely progress.)

C: For the Unexpected — spend 10-15 minutes

"I'll Teach You My Job!"

In the last part of the twice-weekly meeting, we talked about what **has come up unexpectedly** and what people wanted to share.

This part of the meeting is less structured,

but **these discussions are perhaps the most critical part** of what we did in these twice-weekly meetings.

I know you may be asking, "Why?"

They're critical because, they not only give us an "early warning" about what may require our attention…

we came to see that they really are the continuation of the environment scan and SWOT analysis we conducted at the retreat that had focused our work and framed our priorities!

And Watch It Happen Every Day!

D: What Goes on the Calendar

As the calendar is the first part of the twice-weekly meetings,

it's important to develop a clear understanding as to **what information is placed** on the calendar and to what detail.

Listed at the end of this book are the calendar details for new employee orientation as an example of what is put on the calendar.

E: To Put Together a Concrete Deliverable

As it was essential that we evolved our capacity to manage to take on the concrete deliverables,

the following is a great example of a concrete deliverable initiative and how the twice-weekly meeting led to a "best" decision and action.

The critical member of our group on this initiative was Leon because of **the insight he provided** in designing this project and how to execute it.

One of the most critical items that came up during the brainstorming and environmental scan exercises was that we had over **300 missing** I-9 documents for employees.

And Watch It Happen Every Day!
_____

Repeat: This was 300+ missing I-9s for a payroll of some 800 full-time and part-time regular employees — nearly 40% — not a good situation.

Not only are there significant penalties for not having this employment eligibility documentation,

even more important... our failure to get this documentation **undermined the credibility** of the group.

And as departments, other managers, and their employees simply ignored what we required on the I-9s,

it came as no surprise that...

we would also have difficulty getting their assistance and cooperation on other important responsibilities.

"I'll Teach You My Job!"

My efforts to get this information from delinquent employees **weren't very successful...**

Even though the I-9 process required that we not employ an individual who did not provide the information,

the practice of the organization for years had been to not erect a final roadblock to a new employee coming on board who had been selected through a somewhat lengthy recruitment process.

Given the legal obligation, we continued to send requests to these employees requesting they provide the information, but those requests were largely ignored.

And Watch It Happen Every Day!

Finally, in one of our twice-weekly group meetings,

I gave the I-9 status report — that we weren't making much progress.

Leon, who was our records clerk and really had the best knowledge of every personnel transaction and documents, then spoke up.

Usually soft-spoken, he said: **"Let me take care of this."**

And we asked what he would do, and Leon said, "I'll write a letter and you, Ken, have to sign it," and **he'd send it** to every person who was on the non-compliance list.

"I'll Teach You My Job!"

He wrote the letter — I did a few edits and the letter went out.

The letter was direct and straight to the point. It said:

It has come to our attention that you have not provided the required employment eligibility information. Federal law requires that you provide certain documents within three days of the start of your employment.

Failure to do so will result in the termination of your employment. I understand that no one wishes to lose their job, so please bring the information to our office and submit the documents to Leon Hehlen when you arrive at the office.

If the information is not provided, **your employment will** be discontinued effective (date).

And Watch It Happen Every Day!

Upon receiving the letter, a number of employees **made irate** phone calls and they were all directed to Leon.

He calmly told them to bring in the documents and made appointments for each.

Of course, when these employees arrived, many continued to be quite angry, asking to see Leon...

And when Leon came out of the records room to the reception area, **employees who had been quite angry suddenly became** quiet and compliant.

He asked for their documents and they quickly gave them to him and left.

"I'll Teach You My Job!"

You might wonder why?

Could it be that meeting Leon —

> polite and firm and also 6`3" tall and the size of a football defensive tackle… with a firm "look-you-in-the-eye" presence about him that said, "You know what I asked you to provide,"

was a bit of an **unexpected, withering experience?**

Within one month, we had only three employees who hadn't complied and termination actions were submitted for each of them.

And Watch It Happen Every Day!

When they got notice of the pending termination actions, they were also quite angry, but finally appeared with the required documentation...

and in two months, we had gotten all the I-9s and **no longer** had an I-9 problem.

The **post-mortem** on this "What We Wanted to Look Like" initiative:

We all agreed that it was important to take care of this employment eligibility problem.

On a number of occasions, I had brought this to the attention of the organization's leadership and asked for their support,

"I'll Teach You My Job!"

but no one was willing to say explicitly that they wanted this taken care of.

So, **I tried the soft** approach of contacting each employee and asking them to bring in their documentation.

Of course, they didn't.

If it weren't for the group meeting and, in this case, with Leon feeling that he didn't have to defer...

and, as he also knew the problem better than anyone else,

he came up with a solution that we all readily agreed to try.

And Watch It Happen Every Day!

To say what he had put together **was a rousing** success is an understatement.

Yes, I was the "leader" of the group and also the person with final management responsibility,

but Leon clearly demonstrated that he knew how to lead and manage. He did a fabulous job and solved the problem!

I had every confidence in him...

and knew he could **do my job** and he became a high-level HR and management professional in an important public agency.

MAJOR CONSEQUENCES OF THE TWICE-WEEKLY MEETINGS

It should come therefore as no surprise that an important benefit of the twice-weekly meetings was a **heightened level** of engagement and collaboration for those in the group.

People came to realize that they were more effective because the group enabled them to work in ways that they couldn't do alone.

As I said previously, I didn't run these meetings,

and because the practice (the actual "doing") of being in charge of the meetings **built the skills** and confidence of those in the leadership role,

And Watch It Happen Every Day!
_____

it made "real" the responsibility to problem-solve —

to think and then decide, facilitate/organize and importantly to execute which are **essential pieces** for effective management and leadership.

But in addition to providing the leadership opportunity...

because these meetings also led to increased communications as well as coordination among all members...

>again, as it was not unusual to have a group member share information on a similar or related problem or situation (that s/he had also been working with the same individual...

particularly when discussing issues or challenges that just came up...

these twice-weekly meetings led to a much better understanding of each other's work, **how the work each** of us was doing had impact on others, and to see how seemingly separate issues were linked and were part of a larger problem.

Finally, and quite unexpectedly, there were other positive outcomes/benefits that occurred because of these meetings:

One of the best outcomes of these meetings was **that they became self-sustaining**.

And Watch It Happen Every Day!

We all know how often meetings get canceled because the leader is absent —

>away for another meeting or some other professional obligation or perhaps is on vacation,

with adverse results such as the following:

1. We don't get the feedback/perspective and insight from others; issues or questions that someone might have don't get raised or addressed;

2. Items that need attention **instead get delayed** and get pushed down the list because other important and urgent issues come up;

3. And without full information, **we act prematurely or without sufficient information...**

>and can easily head off in the wrong direction where

"I'll Teach You My Job!"

mistakes can be made compounding the problem rather than fixing the problem.

But because there was an agenda for each of these meetings — a calendar and an ongoing set of items, people still met **whether I was** there or not.

They knew the format for the meetings, the agenda was clear, and there was a person in the leadership role.

The group therefore was able to **keep on task** to assure that the necessary work was getting done.

When problems occurred, they were able to redirect and get on course quickly thereby avoiding delays, possible mistakes, and a lot of rework.

Think they didn't know my job?

And Watch It Happen Every Day!

A Final Comment

You may have noted throughout these books that I never talked about performance and the typical periodic or annual assessment of the work that people do.

Building upon what we were doing in our daily work as driven through the twice-weekly meetings...

the widespread practices in performance management found in most organizations and businesses simply were not necessary.

Here's why:

"I'll Teach You My Job!"

While it was **not planned** —

Again, there was no prior template to follow or adopt...

we came to understand that performance should not be seen as a problem...

for which a performance management program (with periodic/annual reviews) is usually seen as the solution,

but **as an outcome of how effective organizations function and/or are managed.**

That is, if we know each day/week or over any period of time what we have done and how well we have done it,

when we look back,

And Watch It Happen Every Day!

we will be looking at what we know we have done well, with assessing performance therefore **being less** of a daunting challenge.

Again, for us as managers and supervisors and executives,

to the extent that we tend to manage similarly —

the twice-weekly meetings not being the norm...

should it come as a surprise that we struggle/face challenges with performance management?

"I'll Teach You My Job!"

Let's now turn our attention to the content of "I'll Teach You My Job."

To plan and organize and to reduce the likelihood of excluding/overlooking a task or event — the omission of which could result in something not being done in a timely manner — requires the clear articulation of preparatory and follow-up activities as in this example of a list of activities for scheduling a monthly new employee orientation:

New employee orientation is held once a month. Invitations are sent to all employees who are to receive health and retirement benefits.

- Overall:
    At least six months in advance of the first orientation event:
    Schedule the upcoming one-year block of monthly orientation sessions with new hires — dates and time.

And Watch It Happen Every Day!

- *At the same time:*
    Also lock-in the room to be used for these orientation sessions for the full-year of orientation sessions.

- *After rooms and dates are set up:*
    Enter room and date and time information for each orientation session in the calendar.

- *Six weeks prior to the scheduled monthly orientation session:*
    Reconfirm the availability of the room at the desired date and time.

- *Five weeks to two weeks prior to the scheduled monthly orientation session:*
    Obtain the names of new hires to be invited to the orientation. For each new hire, will need contact information: name, title, work address, home address, email address and a phone number.

- *Two weeks prior to the scheduled monthly orientation session:*
    Check that all materials to be included in the orientation packet are available;

order/prepare/obtain materials as needed.

- *Two weeks prior to the scheduled monthly orientation session:*
  Send email to all new hires reminding them of the orientation meeting and requesting a confirmation that each will attend; cc to the supervisor/manager.

- *One week prior to the scheduled monthly orientation session:*
  Check the list of new hires against those confirming attendance at orientation.

  Send reminder email to any unconfirmed new hire again requesting confirmation.

  Loop as necessary with a phone call.

  Those unable to attend are scheduled for a subsequent orientation meeting.

- *Three days prior to the scheduled monthly orientation session:*
  Prepare orientation packets against a checklist of items —

And Watch It Happen Every Day!

including a pen/pad of paper, name tent for each new hire also indicating department/work unit.

- *Three days prior to the scheduled monthly orientation session:*
    Place order for refreshments and schedule delivery —location, date, and time.

- *One day prior to the scheduled monthly orientation session:*
    Visit the orientation room and assure that the room is in working order.

- *One day prior to the scheduled monthly orientation session:*
    Assure the computer, any slide decks/video, sound, and projection system (including screen and connectors) are in working order.

- *One day prior to the scheduled monthly orientation session:*
    Confirm that refreshments are ordered and scheduled for delivery at the correct location, date, and time.

"I'll Teach You My Job!"

- *One day prior to the scheduled monthly orientation session:*
    - *Review/rehearse and modify as needed the script for the orientation.*

- *Orientation day:*
    - *Arrive 30 to 45 minutes early to set up computer, distribute packets/materials; prepare the room – seating, chairs, screens, flipchart.*

- *Attendee check-in and follow up for those not attending to schedule for the next orientation session.*

Some might think that the amount of detail for activities on the calendar is considerable. However, as the goal is to assure that nothing is overlooked, this level of detail enables any individual to step in and conduct necessary activities.

Note: If an office or work group chooses to flow chart or process map various activities or processes, that documentation can be readily attached to the calendar as well.

And Watch It Happen Every Day!

Books 9 and 10

"Revisiting Our Jobs So That We Ensure Astounding Success"

Book 9 — "Teaching My Job... A Revisit to Struggling, Magic, and BAM! Even More Lightning Bolts~

Book 9.1 — Teaching My Job... Managing Themes and a Set of Current Plus Two New Activities."

Book 9.2 — Teaching My Job... To Manage Well, Add Two More — the Third and Fourth — Activities Not Usually Discussed

Book 10 – Are We Done Yet? No, We're Just Beginning... The Concrete Deliverables for Building Extraordinary Organizational Capacity

The Appendix: A Commentary on How This Book Is Written

Book 9 — "Teaching My Job... A Revisit to Struggling, Magic, and BAM! Even More Lightning Bolts!"

This is the payoff book – actually two books 9.1 and 9.2

"I'll Teach You My Job!" and BAM! Everything comes together!

>Book 9.1 — Teaching My Job... Managing Themes and a Set of Current Plus Two New Activities

>Book 9.2 — Teaching My Job... To Manage Well, Add Two More — the Third and Fourth — Activities Not Usually Discussed

And Watch It Happen Every Day!

The following is the introduction to Books 9.1 and 9.2 of the ninth book.

I can't say that what I described in the previous books is what you should also do. But I know that I made these changes because what I had learned to do **my job as a manager wasn't working.**

And If you've had similar experiences in your career and would like to get a comprehensive grasp of what I did/changed, read this book.

Book 9 has four parts organized into two books —Book 9.1 with three parts and Book 9.2 with one part. *Each part has a particular focus and aggregately they comprise what I would teach as my job.*

Book 9.1: The first part *is a discussion of four foundational themes that enabled myself and those working with and for me to get on the same page, leading them to become highly effective.*

Book 9.1: The second part *talks about how the three activities — which every group, team or organization is expected to do — can be done at a considerably more effective level. The message is you and your group can do your work well and do it right.*

Book 9.1: The third part. *However, as important as those three activities are, focusing on only those activities overlooks the importance of managing.* **This third part lays out new activities** *that a manager has to do — by overcoming obstacles that limit the effectiveness of those who work with and for us — that will assure enduring viability and success.*

Book 9.2: The fourth part. *While the first three parts of Book 9.1 will raise productivity, to manage well so that a manager does not fall short or possibly fail, this fourth part talks about* **two final activities not usually discussed** *that a manager, a supervisor, or an executive may well want to consider.*

And Watch It Happen Every Day!

Book 9.1 — Teaching My Job... Managing Themes and a Set of Current Plus Two New Activities

PART ONE: FOUR FOUNDATIONAL THEMES

Whether you're **reading this book for the first time...** or you are someone who has worked with and for me,

knowing the following four themes is important because they are the essential foundation for what I did in my job.

"I'll Teach You My Job!"

1. **Breaking through** the unspoken but real limitations of the employer-employee mindset.

2. **Having the commitment** to make those who work with and for me/you so good that others will want to hire them!

3. Recognizing that those who worked with and for me — **who know their jobs better** than I ever would — can also articulate how best to improve their effectiveness.

4. **Leveraging the positive impact** of the "employee-as-leader!"

These themes which got my head in the right place, need to be understood...

because without them as anchors for my thinking,

And Watch It Happen Every Day!

I would never have gone from a struggling manager who had no idea what was going on —

> a manager who couldn't say I was leading or managing...

to a manager who had great working relationships with a great group of people who **became highly effective and did so magically — seemingly overnight!**

The First Theme:

You now know that I had discarded the employer-employee mindset —

"I'll Teach You My Job!"

the prevailing approach to managing found in nearly every organization where,

whether I have a job as a manager, supervisor, director or executive,

I'm in charge because I know best and direct your work...

not just because operating under that mindset had not led to great results, but that mindset created a pervasive, widespread, unwelcome, and subtly negative effect every day,

an artificial, unnecessary distance

that adversely affected the relationships I had with those who worked with and for me.

And Watch It Happen Every Day!

The Second Theme:

That once I had made that commitment...

"to make you so good others would want to hire you!"

instead of seeing your work contributions... as well as the contributions of anyone who worked with and for me,

as being defined and therefore limited by whatever daily duties and activities might be written up in a job description,

again, a prevailing practice utilized by most organizations and businesses,

I was able to see... because you can lead and manage —

capacities which you had gotten because you were using them...

to proactively shape your personal lives outside of work,

that not only were we able to deliver expected services and to effectively respond to ever-changing problems and challenges,

we also saw our relationships magically transform from hierarchical and directive... **to collegial, collaborative, and communicative!**

And Watch It Happen Every Day!

And, as a result, not only I, but everyone in our group, in coming to know on a daily basis what each other was doing...

where we minimized our mistakes and delays which quickly got us on top of the work we were supposed to do...

had become supportive of each other,

and thus we were able to do that work surprisingly well!

The Third Theme:

You should have also come to understand **when I had that lightning bolt experience,**

suddenly realizing that you also know better than I ever would the obstacles that impede your/our operational effectiveness...

as well as the challenges that were adversely impacting us in the workplace,

that together, you and I would also be able to develop and put in place solutions to resolve these problems that limited/inhibited our effectiveness.

The Fourth Theme:

And Watch It Happen Every Day!

That by your stepping forward in the "employee as leader" role, not only did we get on the same page...

with everyone being fully involved on a daily basis — in meaningful activities tied directly to the work each person did each day,

we also **built a unique enduring strength...**

becoming a strongly engaged group of people working together that would never have happened any other way!

We seldom had to deal with that pervasive problem found in most organizations and businesses...

the problem of the unengaged, disengaged and/or toxic, egregiously bad individuals or managers who adversely affect the workplace and our individual and collective productivity.

However, there were situations where I, as the manager with administrative and legal authority, did remove certain individuals when the person failed to contribute/perform.

PART TWO: THREE ACTIVITIES

With those four fundamental themes as a backdrop, **I would then teach that there are three activities that need to be done well.**

The First Activity:

And Watch It Happen Every Day!

The basics and how critical they are...

because **you simply can't be a better manager** and certainly won't be an outstanding manager

if you don't know what's going on and those who work with and for you are not on top of the operational.

The Second Activity:

I would then teach that it is **important to remove the egregiously bad** because they create an adverse work environment which not only distracts others from doing their best work,

they also drive away the best people — a cost no organization or business can accept.

The Third Activity:

What I would teach next is that it is essential to focus on the **"The What We Want to Look Like"**...

because putting together concrete deliverables that move our group and the organization forward is how we can "shape the future."

These three activities...

doing our expected work well,

improving the workplace and the culture of the organization,

and positioning ourselves/the organization for viability and on-going success

And Watch It Happen Every Day!

are the essentials that any manager should know/focus on so that a group or team will be doing the work that counts.

PART THREE: GOING BEYOND THE FOUR FOUNDATIONAL THEMES AND THE THREE ACTIVITIES AND COMING TO GRIPS WITH MY JOB! NEW ACTIVITIES

The four foundational themes that were discussed as the first part above were important because they got my head in the right place…

The three activities that followed in the second part were important because, if they're done well, they collectively assured a strong level of performance.

"I'll Teach You My Job!"

However, despite the positives from the themes and these activities, **I had a feeling** that something more had to be done...

And what was that?

What had to be taken care of was...

what **I would do to reconcile** those four themes and three activities that had led to changing my relationship with those who worked with and for me...

with what I would be doing in my job...

Because, so long as you/those who worked with and for me...

And Watch It Happen Every Day!

---

did not know my job and what I was doing,

we would not be in sync,

and this chasm —

> a barrier to communications, ideas, and solutions between the work you were doing and that I was doing...

would limit our collective effectiveness.

So, even though I realized that teaching my job would be the key to syncing up your work with my work,

"I'll Teach You My Job!"

instead of feeling this was a positive development…

I had a rather unsettling discomfort — vague at first — that just wouldn't go away.

And as I sought "to come to grips" with this unease, **it became glaringly obvious** what the source was of my discomfort.

My discomfort came from… the fact that by your now using your capacities to lead and to manage

and therefore to oversee and organize activities, such as

- our operational work and related processes,

- the calendar and deadlines,

And Watch It Happen Every Day!

- our challenges in the workplace,

- and initiatives related to "What We Wanted to Look Like"

all of which were being done through our twice-weekly meetings which you were also leading,

I simply no longer had those direct responsibilities!

And since I no longer had those responsibilities, **I had come face-to-face** with the unavoidable conclusion that…

since what had been my job was no longer what I was doing,

"I'll Teach You My Job!"

what exactly was now my job?

This concern about my job brought back those anxieties and frustrations reminiscent of what I had experienced in Book 1 when I didn't know what others were doing…

Except now, this was even more intense — **this time it was different** because rather than being about not knowing what others were doing,

this time it was about me!

And as I realized that I had to answer that same question as to what my job was — and **particularly what I would be doing on a daily basis…**

And Watch It Happen Every Day!

- What was I doing every day that one would called leading and managing?

- What would I be doing every day that was in sync with what the group/team was doing?

- What would I be doing every day to contribute/help drive our greater productivity and effectiveness?

I realized that,

if I couldn't say what the work was that I was doing on a daily basis...

why was I — or any other manager or director or executive — **needed?**

However, after getting over this initial shock that I hadn't addressed what my job was now...

because I felt that I was still doing important work...

even though what those activities were in my job was not yet apparent,

I concluded that I hadn't managed myself into obsolescence.

So, I backed up to get some perspective, something which I think every manager who sees the positive benefits of teaching his/her job,

and had the following thought come to mind.

Because it was important that I and those who work with and for me be in sync, it was essential that **what I did each day... had to strongly tie** to/have direct impact on the work being done by those who work with and for me.

And Watch It Happen Every Day!

Now, I recognize that some might think it's **not essential to have our work** be in sync so closely...

After all, don't I have the responsibilities to provide strategic direction and so forth as the person in-charge?

> that is, isn't there some validity to what we've always been told are our responsibilities as managers, supervisors, or executives,

> so why should I change and take on new activities...

But, if that's your view,

I ask that you look at the following typical list for those of us who are "in charge" and ask yourself... as I did...

"I'll Teach You My Job!"

if it is your sense that these describe your responsibilities in your job,

what is it exactly that you would be doing every day...

that directly ties to/has daily impact on the work being done by those who report to you?

- I am responsible for the development and administration of a set of programs and services,

- **I plan and strategize** and by keeping on top of developments/trends related to those programs and services,

- **I set the vision/direction and priorities,**

- I am responsible for organizing what needs to be done, directing others to take on certain tasks and responsibilities.

And Watch It Happen Every Day!

- **I also assess progress,** conducting periodic assessments to determine what's impeding our progress and also make adjustments and changes as needed,

- I provide coaching as necessary or requested,

- I produce reports and provide information to be disseminated to others,

and

- **I also take the lead** to develop projects and undertake other initiatives as needed or directed.

As I thought about each of these responsibilities and realized that it was difficult to say what I would be doing every day for each of these responsibilities,

"I'll Teach You My Job!"

BAM!

what popped into my head was **this was not a list** of the kind of responsibilities that should be the focus of my work.

And, as I remembered that commitment...

to "make those who worked with and for me so good that others would want to hire them,"

it all fell into place and I knew what was essential in the work I would do in my job.

THE NEW ACTIVITIES IN MY JOB:

And Watch It Happen Every Day!

Remember the idea that good managers get things done through people?

It's absolutely true.

If people don't have the right equipment or aren't trained correctly… or don't have the right processes or working relationships that will enable them to work well with others,

not only would they not be as successful as they might be, what I would want to see accomplished as a manager would not happen either!

However, even though we know that what I just wrote makes sense,

"I'll Teach You My Job!"

I also know that we as managers and executives don't always act accordingly.

We tend to think that people who are having difficulties with their daily work... will figure out how best to cope with their circumstances.

After all, their smarts were why we hired the people we brought on board.

So, as we expect that they'll just work through this... somehow putting up with the inconveniences/hassles, they will still get their work done.

And in most cases, we might well be right.

But there's an important question which we never really answer:

And Watch It Happen Every Day!

Is that really our responsibility?

Is it really a part of our job...

where does it say in our job descriptions that we are to let people cope with something that impedes their work and effectiveness...

where we do little if anything?

We all know intellectually that this would be unacceptable.

But since we really don't understand what to do...

in part because we don't know what they're doing on a daily basis,

here's something I think would help us understand what we should do if helping others succeed is a responsibility for those of us "in charge."

Take a simple step back and put yourself in their shoes.

Think of your experiences as a mid-level or higher manager or even if you are a division head or a vice-president or even a CEO.

Haven't you been just uplifted when your boss or the board did something for you? When s/he/they simply were able to make something happen that you couldn't through your own efforts —

And Watch It Happen Every Day!
___

- like getting more positions;

- coming up with the money to support your request to buy the right technology;

- giving you funds to buy equipment;

- to bring in a consultant or to hire some special expertise that would make a difference;

- or convincing other higher-level executives that s/he worked and interacted with to make decisions that addressed and helped you resolve/overcome a particular problem or challenge you were facing/struggling with.

- or opening certain doors.

Didn't those actions that your boss took
and maybe really didn't need to — make your job a lot easier?

"I'll Teach You My Job!"

Didn't those actions/resources make it **possible for you to succeed?**

So, if that's the case for you, why isn't that the case also for those who work with and for you?

Don't you think they'd be able to do their jobs better? **Don't you think that** they'd succeed if you took steps…

if you took actions and made decisions as a manager — or as a supervisor, a division head, or as an executive that would enable them to be more productive and effective?

Of course, **the answer is YES!**

So why aren't we doing that?

And Watch It Happen Every Day!

The answer is… **none of us have been taught** —

none of us think that it is our job to enable those who work with and for us to succeed!

We think it's enough that we've hired them, paid them a salary or a wage, and given them a set of duties in their job descriptions… (the employer-employee mindset!)

Yet, if that is what our job really is…

>   the job of any manager, supervisor or executive…

>   which, if we don't do, increases the likelihood of failure,

"I'll Teach You My Job!"

but instead we explicitly see our role as enabling the success of those who work with and for us,

we also will likely succeed... and, importantly, collectively we may also...

MAKE A CRITICAL DIFFERENCE IN THE SUCCESS AND VIABILITY OF OUR ORGANIZATION/BUSINESS!

Of course, it was great to realize this overarching purpose of my job which was to enable the success of others —

but as this was just a concept,

And Watch It Happen Every Day!

I also knew, because of what I had experienced when I had just started in a managing job,

that if my work were to have impact,

it was absolutely essential that what I did in practice — at work every day **had to be part of and in sync** with those who work with and for me!

And, again, that BIG glaring light bulb went on!

As I had written earlier in this Book 9,

"I'll Teach You My Job!"

even though those working with and for me had assumed responsibilities to lead and to manage on operational and workplace matters as well as "The What We Want to Look Like,"

and even though they were highly motivated,

I realized, as their work was limited to what they do as part of their daily work, **it was therefore impractical —**

given the nature of organizational realities,

that those who are professionals and/or primarily have technical/administrative support responsibilities...

would be able to undertake/handle effectively on a daily basis certain management activities...

And Watch It Happen Every Day!

activities such as

engaging in appointments and meeting on a regularly scheduled or on an as-needed basis with my counterparts — other managers or directors,

or with a division head/vice-president outside of our own/their own area...

and, for sure,

these individuals/groups would not be holding ongoing working meetings with the CEO.

Even though **as managers we lament/express** some frustration about having to

"I'll Teach You My Job!"

spend our time in these meetings —

because we think that these meetings consume too much of our time — like 75% of our day...

But, again, take that step back.

When you think about these meetings and what transpires in them — such as the discussions that would not occur in any other venue or occasion,

you have to realize that these meetings are important and have value...

that they are necessary and **are core to our jobs.**

And Watch It Happen Every Day!

And why are they so essential?

As I said above — while we as managers often bemoan these meetings and discussions, **we also have to recognize,**

as these are important activities that "employers as leaders" can't easily do...

that our being in these meetings and participating in these discussions with others **are truly a core purpose** and activity of our jobs,

because they are the opportunities to address and resolve issues... that will enable us to bring about the success of those who work with and for us.

"I'll Teach You My Job!"

Viewed thusly, it becomes clear that **our participation is vital —**

that I was not just participating in those meetings and discussions because I/we had to!

I came to see by being part of those sessions that

it became possible to do things that are certainly beyond "employees as leaders"… but may also be beyond my own capacity to do on my own.

And because there are such positive benefits that could come from these sessions,

> while you may not agree with what I've written on the following pages or may want to suggest as different activities,

And Watch It Happen Every Day!
___

I realized that to be successful as a manager my job now had **two new activities that would be the drivers** of my managerial work.

And, again, recognizing that "employees as leaders" could not undertake these activities on a daily basis,

rather than meeting to talk and exchange information, **I went into these meetings...**

>whether they were meetings that I had organized or attended —

>a minimum of five to sometimes up to ten times every day,

"I'll Teach You My Job!"

focused on finding resources that people who work with and for me needed to make them more effective and productive!

Sometimes I simply needed more money to hire the right people with the right talent/skills.

Sometimes it was even more basic... and we all know this, I just needed more people.

> people who had minimal skills but who either I or the managers/supervisors could train and get up to speed.

And sometimes...

because of the extraordinary workloads that people were having to deal with

And Watch It Happen Every Day!

each day, people were just too busy, they were burning out…

And when you don't have enough people, **they will make mistakes —**

>they won't check/recheck their work…

>and bad data gets into the system or data aren't entered at all.

>or the part won't be used properly, something isn't done to specification, or what was supposed to be fixed doesn't work.

So sometimes, **what we needed was a piece of technology.**

And, again, technology is a great example of the impact of finding resources.

Later in my career, in a different office we had a set of **60 documents that were routinely submitted as well as receiving numerous requests each day.**

And with documents/requests coming from hundreds of employees/colleagues, the workload was such that we weren't tracking who had submitted the document or made the request and to whom the document/request was to be given.

We were simply too busy,

just trying to get through the day, and, in the case of documents, whenever we received one of those,

And Watch It Happen Every Day!

it was date-stamped and the person —

usually **an individual in an entry level position** who was just beginning to acquire some amount of knowledge and experience —

did their best to decide into whose inbox the document or message would be placed.

Routing documents may sound simple, but the volume of up to sixty different types of documents being possibly sent to 40+ people makes clear why documents would get lost.

"I'll Teach You My Job!"

This was a perfect storm. With the document not being logged in and in failing to track to whom the document had been sent, the result was inevitable, predictable, and understandable...

a constant stream — oftentimes a torrent — of daily complaints, angry inquiries and criticisms regarding documents that had been submitted but not processed...

that had been processed incorrectly... or that had been lost because we didn't even know to whom the document had been given.

While I and others could fight the episodic battle each day to find the missing document

or make sure to correct each instance where the data had been entered incorrectly or to locate a missing document,

And Watch It Happen Every Day!

doing so would mean that **I — and everyone else — were caught in that unending "Whack A Mole!" —**

trying to find the "mishandled" documents that we had received.

Because we didn't have a log of ever having received those documents and thus weren't able to get on top of what we needed to do, what did people work on?

They put extraordinary effort working on the documents that were being placed on their desk that day or the requests they were receiving,

but they also worked on finding the document or request that had triggered a complaint!

"I'll Teach You My Job!"

(Sometimes unfortunately setting aside a document they didn't know what to do with.)

And, in spending hours looking for that missing piece of paper or trying to figure out why something which had supposedly been taken care of hadn't been completed...

It was no surprise that people were burning out.

Recognizing that we couldn't continue to work this way on a daily basis because of the toll on people and the adverse impact on our relationship with our clients,

I turned to technology.

And Watch It Happen Every Day!

And the rationale for looking at technology was to provide a systematic procedure that would remedy the problems with the manual process we had been using.

As I discussed the situation with a number of people, one individual said that **he was familiar with the system** I was talking about...

>a system which, by the way, had an annual fee of $150,000...

and, since I knew from discussions with our chief financial officer that **we couldn't afford such a fee,**

Sandolin and Etrell, another IT professional who became quite engaged in the project, over the next four months did the programming to build that system and **we had our solution!**

"I'll Teach You My Job!"

The system that was able to track every document or a request we received as well as to whom the document/request had been sent.

A system that also sent emails to the client as well as provided reminders to the person who had received the document as well as to the individual's manager!

So, as this example of the impact of technology illustrates,

finding resources is essential... because it enables our people to have success.

It is a task that I —

And Watch It Happen Every Day!

and any other person who is a manager, a supervisor, a director, administrative, team leader, section head or vice president —

have to recognize as a unique, essential responsibility of our jobs!

So, if finding resources was the first activity... **what was the second new activity?**

As much as we've been told that organizations and businesses are well-organized,

>that their activities are aligned with a common purpose, mission, or a business plan — working toward achieving a set of common goals,

"I'll Teach You My Job!"

---

the reality is that operations have bumps and hurdles that impede our work every day.

Some are simply built-in because of the different procedures and policies used and we may not be sufficiently familiar with them — for example, in finance, in IT...

We know these policies, programs, these long-standing practices are just part of daily work in our businesses and organizations.

The problem is when **we try to implement something new...** or to strengthen an existing program or service,

And Watch It Happen Every Day!

we sometimes can meet the substantial obstacle of inertia — where what you or I want to do or change is not the way business is done.

We know that it's not that anyone is adamantly or even slightly opposed.

But even if it is apparent that such change will be beneficial/meaningful to others, those with their authorities and responsibilities will look to existing policy, procedure, or established practice...

and **not act as expeditiously as we would like.**

I'll give you an example from a project I had worked on as a consultant... an experience I'm sure most of us have had.

"I'll Teach You My Job!"

The head of a major department **had submitted documents to adjust the pay**

for a group of higher-performing employees that this administrator had found to be in the lower half of the comparable market data.

What ensued was a number of intense phone calls and emails… followed by the back-and-forth of requests to submit clarifying information or to provide "missing documentation."

While these conversations and revisions of materials submitted resulted in some delay,

there was a policy that was the key obstacle.

And Watch It Happen Every Day!

The policy allowed for up to 60 days for a request to be processed.

And in most cases, the time taken to process those requests **nearly without exception took all of those 60 days that the policy allowed!**

The time being taken had become so frustrating that the vice-president of the division called me directly, even though I wasn't in charge of the people doing this work.

Obviously, this was a problem and, even though I was a consultant,

I did follow up and, after verifying the process and the time being taken for these requests, I met with

"I'll Teach You My Job!"

the appropriate people and **submitted a report regarding the problem.**

The policy wasn't changed, **but the practice of using close to the number of days that the policy allowed was halted.**

Whether you're a manager or, in my case, a consultant, that long-standing practice had imposed an inertia,

an inertia that was an obstacle that had to be removed.

As I said, I did work on this problem in my consulting role, **but, if you're a manager, supervisor, division head —**

And Watch It Happen Every Day!

the clear message is that we use **those meetings...** which we attend and participate in every day, **and go into them to remove obstacles.**

Because in doing so, **what YOU want...** which is to enhance the success of those who work with and for us or for those who work for someone else

will in fact happen!

As I know that these two activities – finding resources and clearing away obstacles, are not typically found in the job description of a manager, supervisor, division head or an executive,

"I'll Teach You My Job!"

it's understandable that you may want to hold onto the standard duties and responsibilities that are found in our job descriptions.

But realize, as those duties and responsibilities which I had described earlier in this book…

simply do not say anything about what **you would do on a daily basis to make others successful,**

holding on to thinking that these job descriptions define what your job is…

will keep you where you are.

And Watch It Happen Every Day!

That is, **as they do not tie your work** to the work being done by those who work with and for you,

those duties and responsibilities will create that "pervasive, unwelcome" distance — that chasm that will separate you from your people doing the work.

And,

as therefore you and your group/team/office will not be in sync... **and as you also won't** have strong collaborative relationships where you're on the same page with the same priorities...

relying on those long-standing duties and responsibilities will lead to your falling short and failing,

"I'll Teach You My Job!"

and your continuing to be average as a manager!

And Watch It Happen Every Day!

Book 9.2 — Teaching My Job... To Manage Well, Add Two More — the Third and Fourth — Unique Activities Not Usually Discussed

Realizing that finding resources and removing obstacles were now two new activities of my job...

that were essential to the success of others was an important breakthrough,

BUT THAT WASN'T ALL TO MY JOB...

There were two more unique responsibilities that I, as the person

"in charge" had.

I realized, if you want to manage well — and not just manage,

in additional to finding resources and removing obstacles...

as part of furthering the commitment I had made to the success of others,

that I had to pay attention to the skills and knowledge people needed to do their jobs well!

As I said in previous books that I see it as critical that management effectiveness be demonstrated in and as part of daily work,

And Watch It Happen Every Day!

and also that making change — as when I made the commitment to teach my job — starts with the boss,

it just followed that as part of the work I did on a daily basis,

I had this new third activity…

to assure that **each person was improving every day!**

Did I just hear you say,

as the person in charge that I have the responsibility to assure that each person will improve "every day?"

That's JUST unrealistic…

"I'll Teach You My Job!"

It's hard enough to find time for people to get trained even if we provide the funding to send them to a workshop…

to then say that we should help them improve every day just seems like **a huge, if not impossible, challenge.**

But here are the examples where this happened —

where people have learned a new skill and in doing so have improved every day.

Recall three specific examples which I mentioned earlier in this book:

Flowcharting: I brought in an individual who over the course of three of our meetings taught us how to flowchart.

And Watch It Happen Every Day!

Additionally, I sent two others from my office to learn how to map workflow by attending a three-day workshop on process mapping.

And **with everyone learning** to either flowchart or process map or both,

by now having the skill/knowledge to write up the specific steps/activities for over 30 major work processes over the course of weeks/months,

we minimized/stop making mistakes and learned the importance of detail in workflow...

and importantly to adjust that workflow whenever needed.

And, as a result, we minimized our mistakes with a skill that improved the work being done by each person

"I'll Teach You My Job!"

every day!

The second example of people improving every day was when we **began to take on** the egregiously bad workplace challenges.

I made reference to the fact that I had learned to conduct workplace-related investigations and had used that method to handle the administrator who had been yelling at people in her office.

As I had **found the method** so useful, I subsequently brought to our city the person who had trained me…

and that person conducted two workshops that not only individuals from my group attended,

And Watch It Happen Every Day!
_____

but also 60+ others from various businesses and other organizations also attended.

However, it wasn't the training that was important, essential as it was.

What was important was, as these egregious workplace challenges **were tied to policy,**

and as each person in our group learned about policies that previously they had little reason to know...

> since workplace norms and expectations were normally not articulated on a regular basis or actively enforced.

they realized that policies were key to changing the workplace climate, to changing the culture of the organization,

"I'll Teach You My Job!"

and having learned policies, they found what they needed **to work more effectively** with their colleagues regarding the egregiously bad individuals in the organization!

The third example is how people worked together and learned from each other to take care of their work responsibilities every day.

I had two individuals — as I'm sure everyone does — people who have different expertise.

In my case, I had one individual who knew budget and benefits and other who knew employment.

As these were complementary bodies of knowledge,

And Watch It Happen Every Day!

---

these two individuals talked with each other on a daily basis...

drawing on the insight and experience of the other person to take of the work they had before them and, as needed, to solve an unfamiliar problem.

And as these two individuals explained in the twice-weekly meetings how they were working together,

what happened was that others realized that, as they also had to handle problems outside of their usual area...

> while they could have gone to a workshop outside of the organization to learn,

"I'll Teach You My Job!"

the immediacy of the problem required they deal with the problem/challenge quickly.

Thus, they learned that the best way to get on top of what they needed to know and do… was by talking with their colleagues at work who had handled similar situations.

I came to **call this "site-based training"** because these working sessions/discussions which were daily events where people met to share information

was how they were able to improve every day.

Again, we didn't send people to a workshop or a training session.

They learned what they needed to know in these

And Watch It Happen Every Day!
___

meetings/conversations that took place within our group and our offices on a daily basis!

In addition to this third new activity of helping people improve every day, let's now turn to the fourth activity.

The Fourth Activity:

A New Perspective on What It Takes to Shape the Future

When I thought about what we had accomplished and even though I now had three new responsibilities in my job,

I was still troubled because I knew on occasion that I had fallen short.

Of course, another light bulb went on...

and I experienced a very unusual insight —

one that anyone who is to lead and to manage effectively and to enable the success of others will recognize as important when you read what I've written below.

I realized that **we were able to take on** the problems and challenges related to our operational work and the egregiously bad situations

as well as the "Wanted We Wanted to Look Like"

because we "knew" what we were dealing with!

And Watch It Happen Every Day!

That is, even though these problems and challenges were difficult, **we were able to take those all on because what we had to deal with was "known."**

In fact, they were too well-known — because, as I had written in Book 1, we and others experienced them every day…

>our ineffectiveness operationally and the gut-wrenching disruptions in the workplace.

And, while we had taken on the operational and the egregiously bad and dealt with them…

>accomplishing what any office, group, team, or division would regard as certain adequate if not

quite positive,

the problem was, **if we were to think...**

that resolving problems and challenges that were "known" was "managing well,"

we would simply be unprepared when we came up against the unexpected that just doesn't fit, that pops up and is disruptive.

And, as I recalled situations/problems that we — as managers, supervisors, division heads and even executives, hadn't handle well,

I realized that managing effectively is more than managing the known.

And Watch It Happen Every Day!

Managing well meant we must effectively manage the uncertain, the unexpected.

But wait!

While this is very logical to say that we have to manage the unknown, how can you/someone manage that which you don't know? How does one manage the unknown?

The answer is, we actually do know, but we missed it —

"I'll Teach You My Job!"

And how did we miss it?

We missed it because in our decisions with our focus on our daily work, what we chose to do and how to do it is what led to our missing what was in front of us.

Remember when we did the environmental scan and the SWOT analysis at the retreat(s) – or those exercises that some might call "strategic planning" or putting together a business plan,

and came to understand the more pressing operational problems and challenges in the workplace?

In choosing to focus on certain problems and challenges,

whether we did this explicitly by saying, here's a

And Watch It Happen Every Day!

strength we should utilize —

or by going after what some call **"low-hanging fruit" because they were easier** and more obvious and would demonstrate "progress" —

or by simply assuming and going with what we have done previously, relying on certain individuals or existing programs that in the past had led to success which we felt would likely work again,

we made understandably reasonable choices.

That, in having experienced success previously and **therefore being confident** that this would likely work again,

"I'll Teach You My Job!"

we decided what we should focus on…

and by these choices, we decided that there was no need to deal with/address our weaknesses and the threats that might be out there.

The problem is, of course, those threats don't go away…

and, as long as we continue to remain unaware of the uncertain, the unknown —

> because we have pushed them into the background,

it should come as no surprise that we would be unprepared to deal with them when they did emerge/arise.

And Watch It Happen Every Day!

Understanding that these problems/challenges — our weaknesses and the threats we face **don't go away,**

and because we're not prepared for them, it's clear why we would fall short, maybe even fail — and **experience setbacks that would limit our efforts to shape** the future we had envisioned.

So, in addition to teaching that in my job I had to find resources, to remove obstacles that impede the success of those working with...

and to assure that we improved every day,

I also saw that it was imperative... if we as managers are to manage well and therefore to enable those who work with and for us to be successful, that I had to teach the importance of paying attention/being mindful of the exposure or risks related to our being negligent about/being blind to weaknesses and threats — **the "unknown."**

While you might agree that what I just wrote makes sense, I know when I had to deal with the "unknown," it wasn't easy.

As a manager (supervisor or executive), **asking me to** be prepared to deal with "unknowns" was too abstract.

It's just easier for me and those who work with and for me to make decisions and do the activities that keep us on track… and that will minimize/take care of the

And Watch It Happen Every Day!

adverse consequences of "known" problems and challenges....

And, as I would like to similarly handle the "unknown," what I need to know is: **What are these unknowns?**

And, of course, **the unsatisfactory answer** is that we don't have an inventory of them... **there is no definitive list.**

But what I found helpful was when I realized that...

as it is impossible to predict whether failure occurs due to internal and external threats, weaknesses, and/or the unexpected,

for me to be effective in my job — to manage well,

"I'll Teach You My Job!"

---

what I should teach as a core activity of my job is that we need to be aware that these unpredictable unknowns are always out there,

and that **we should stop managing** in ways that lead us to not see them.

That I, as the manager, supervisor, director, or executive, need to provide the leadership **that will make us — as well as those who work with and for us — aware** that we should no longer ignore these unpredictable unknowns,

but discuss the topic of threats, weaknesses, and unknowns openly… and do so every day.

Because once we know we can deal with the "unknown;" that is, threats that we had chosen to

And Watch It Happen Every Day!

ignore,

we might find that we are able to do what is needed to "shape the future!"

As dealing with the "unknown" can be a difference-maker,

I am going to share an example which we all know that will make the point...

and, as it's an example that those of us who are in charge may find somewhat uncomfortable, it will take a willingness to not over-react, but to read and contemplate,

and if you agree, to then act.

I believe that we who are in these management and leadership

positions...

can recognize that this issue which hasn't been raised/has been avoided as too challenging

is a key to raising productivity and performance...

and it is critical to address.

And once we understand that this threat/unknown can be dealt with,

doing so can have amazing positive impact.

So what is this unpredictable unknown...

And Watch It Happen Every Day!
___

one which is not handled well, and which some will be reluctant to discuss —

that is found in nearly all organizations or businesses?

It is, we always have a sense...

regardless of the level of our position,

we have an unease that those to whom we report — those who review and evaluate us —

may not have that commitment to make us successful!

"I'll Teach You My Job!"

And, because too many of us have had "the errors of our ways" pointed out — because for some reason we didn't do things up to expectations...

falling short of expectations which may not have been clear,

it often means, in having chosen to stand back and then judge and criticize,

that we who are in charge don't have that commitment or haven't told those who work with and for us that I/we/you have such a commitment...

that they have not realized that it is our responsibility...

and that we/you/they also don't know it is our self-interest to take the steps —

And Watch It Happen Every Day!

to act and find resources and remove obstacles — **to enable us/people to succeed!**

Historically, we've called this the "Peter Principle."

But maybe this view is wrong.

The problem isn't that people have somehow bumped up against/reached their top potential.

The problem is that those to whom we report — **don't realize that they can do things...**

that they have a responsibility to take steps/make decisions that will enable us who report to them to be

"I'll Teach You My Job!"

successful!

Because the simple fact is... if we don't succeed, it is highly likely those to whom we report won't succeed either.

So, if we're "in charge," doesn't it make sense...

to tell those who report to us that we're committed to their success and that we would take the steps needed to enable their success?

Again, this is very different.

I know that those who are "in charge" will not necessarily agree with this.

And Watch It Happen Every Day!

But, as this failure/reluctance on the part of those in charge is indicative of a lack of awareness and knowledge regarding what it takes to succeed…

it really is a "A BIG DEAD MOOSE."

But while this one is not directly egregiously bad like the other dead moose… its effects are nonetheless similar.

If you as the boss don't take proactive steps to help those who work with and for you to succeed, **the adverse impact will be…**

> to undermine morale in the workplace,

> to make people question why they would want to stay,

"I'll Teach You My Job!"

to likely drive the best people away.

and what's worse, to undermine what we say as an organization or a business that we stand for.

That is, while we who are in charge may not intend this...

by not enabling others to success contributes directly to creating an adverse culture.

And even if we now understand that this is a **BIG DEAD MOOSE**,

we need to realize that...

this one is even more difficult because,

And Watch It Happen Every Day!
___

while it appears to be more subtle... perhaps never having surfaced before,

or being in the back of all of our minds,

it is even harder — for those in charge and for those who report to these individuals – to acknowledge and know what to do...

But we know the solution.

Again, this goes back to "It all starts with the boss."

And if you're in charge and choose not to act,

doing so is probably **one of the biggest reasons** for falling short and perhaps your individual failure...

as well as contributing to the falling short/failure of the organization or business.

So, what to do?

It's like all other deliverables. Once you've read about it, it is no longer an "unknown" but it is a threat and a "known" threat.

And once we perceive it as a threat, we will surface it, and then act, **and not be "blindsided" with significant adverse consequences.**

And Watch It Happen Every Day!
_____

If you're the person in charge – whether you're a manager, supervisor, team leader, division head, or a CEO/President, making a commitment to succeed to every person who reports to you is essential.

However, there is a simple litmus test. If you find that you cannot make that commitment to an individual, then you have a major decision to make whether you should be retaining that individual.

And for those of us who report to someone, realize that if that commitment to your success isn't forthcoming, wisdom would say find another place to work and decisively take the steps to do so quickly.

So, as has been said in other parts of this book...

if you, as the person in charge, can make this commitment to the success of those who work with and for you, and remove a large unknown in your group or company...

that is, among those who work with and for you,

you may well raise not only their effectiveness but yours as well to a higher level.

TEACHING MY JOB: THE SUMMARY

So I want to wrap things up...

If you worked with and for me, or even if you didn't but you wanted to learn my job, here's what I would teach.

And Watch It Happen Every Day!

1: Deal with the present – the operational work that we must do well every day.

That is, the basics — the operational work done well because these are critical to being a better manager, supervisor, division head, team lead, executive or CEO —

2: Limit the adverse influence of the egregiously bad.

That is, remove those who have an adverse impact on the work environment that distracts others from doing their best work.

That you recognize that those whose behaviors and attitudes which often drive away the best people **are a cost no organization can accept.**

3: Shape the future to make our workplaces as well as our businesses and organizations better.

Begin with seeing those who worked with and for you/me in their roles as "employees as leaders"…

and then **leverage their capacities to lead and to manage** to develop/put in place "concrete deliverables" through the twice-weekly meetings.

And Watch It Happen Every Day!

4: As the duties and responsibilities of my job have changed,

the litmus test, a new focus of my job that would move me to manage well...

was realizing that it was my responsibility to enable the success of others...

and to enable their success,

I would do this through these new activities of removing obstacles and finding resources as well as by helping people improve every day in their effectiveness.

But, finally, because it is so important,

"I'll Teach You My Job!"

for those of us who are "in charge" —
including those who are employees as leaders —

it is imperative that working on the unknown —

>those threats and weaknesses, the unpredictable, the unanticipated which we had previously chosen to pay not much or not any attention to,

>including the matter of whether we who are in charge have a commitment to those who work with and for us...

must become part of our daily work.

While the unknown — these threats and weaknesses —

And Watch It Happen Every Day!

may be surfaced through various strategizing methods (SWOT, environmental scan, strategic planning),

more often than not, as those efforts,

> which are focused on establishing goals and determining major priorities and how we can best organize our energy and resources to achieve desired ends,

are undertaken only periodically through major activities such as retreats,

we are not prepared for crises and major challenges —

> these unpredictable events which arise whenever and do not happen according to a calendar or fit within our usual approaches to planning.

"I'll Teach You My Job!"

As we therefore run the risk of our falling short if not failing, dealing with the unknown is critical...

and to do this, it is clear that changing management practices is essential

and the best way to do this is **by making addressing the unknown as part of our daily work.**

And, to reiterate,

We tend to see the unknown, the unpredictable, the threats and weaknesses as external.

However, that view blinds us to perhaps the most critical challenge, one is not widely discussed or addressed.

And that challenge is that, we – those of us who are "in

And Watch It Happen Every Day!
_____

charge" – have to recognize that we set the culture of our businesses and organizations...

and that by making a commitment to the success of those who work with and for us,

we can create a positive workplace and therefore a difference...

in the effectiveness of productivity of individuals as well as across our businesses and organizations!

If one wants to manage well,

what I've listed in this summary is what I do and is what I teach.

"I'll Teach You My Job!"

What follows is an Addendum to this book followed by the final Book 10.

This addendum is optional, but if you choose to look at this addendum and answer the questions, you may well come away with a sense of the degree to which you have learned my job — and a better sense as to whether you are prepared "to manage well" and enable the success of others.

And Watch It Happen Every Day!

An Addendum to Book 9
Questions Related to How I Managed

What follows is a series of questions which you as the reader can answer. They will help you further understand what you would learn if I taught you my job.

I consider these questions as optional.

If you wish to not answer these questions, then go to Book 10 — the final book.

There are three sets of questions.

"I'll Teach You My Job!"

PART I — THE "PERSON IN CHARGE"

In this first part, I provide the answers first.

Your task is to match each answer to one of the five questions. For some answers there may not be a matching question; that is, there are more answers than questions.

Here are the answers:

1. *Failure to understand that as the newest person, I actually know the least.*

2. *I will make you so good others will want to hire you!*

3. *Set stretch goals, work with a mentor, retain a professional coach.*

4. *They will let you fail whether by being passively or openly aggressive or by leaving.*

5. *The role of the critic.*

And Watch It Happen Every Day!

6. Another piece of management lore that is engrained in nearly every organization or business is the "employer-employee contract" where we see all who work for you as employees and we, as the employer, hire people to do a job and we pay them for their work.

7. Even though the jobs are different, we take what we thought worked in our previous job(s) and try to use that in our new job!

8. You can't change people. You can only change the way you work with them.

9. People who have bad attitudes and bad behavior are just something we have to put up with.

10. We had to convey somehow what we as a group and this organization stood for so that people could understand… why, beyond a paycheck, should they want to work here?

11. Adults! That's who they were… doesn't it make sense that our organizations and our own productivity as managers will be strengthened… if those very capacities can be brought to bear also on a daily basis

"I'll Teach You My Job!"

at work where they are spending eight or more hours every day?

Question 1: If you disregard the experience and insight of others, what is the role you've left them?

Question 2: What behavior(s) would people exhibit in that role?

Question 3: What is the biggest barrier preventing a manager, supervisor, or executive from seeing the importance of the people who work with and for them?

Question 4: If a manager, supervisor, director, or an executive is less than successful, is seen as average at best and/or falls short or fails, what would you say is the primary reason?

Question 5: If you're a manager, a supervisor, or an executive who realizes that you need to improve your leadership and management effectiveness in order to achieve desired results, what would you do?

And Watch It Happen Every Day!

PART II — WORK RELATIONSHIPS

The first five questions were about the manager, supervisor, or executive — "the person in charge."

But success at work is not just about the person "in charge." Productivity and effectiveness are about our relationships and being on the same page with those who work with and for us.

The next set of questions is intended to bring perspective regarding what leads to work effectiveness.

Using a scale of 1 to 10, with 10 being the best rating, **rate the following seven questions**:

Question 1: As a manager, rate the degree to which the performance evaluations that you've received are a fair representation of your contributions and effectiveness.

Question 2: What is your confidence level of your knowledge as to what each person who works with and for you is doing today, didn't not complete yesterday, and will be focused on tomorrow?

Question 3: As a manager, indicate your level of confidence that the performance evaluations you have given your people are:

Accurate

Meaningful

Useful for Further Development

Question 4: As it is essential to "align" your work as well as the work of your people, rate your knowledge of your boss' goals, priorities, and expectations.

Question 5: As a manager or an executive, rate your level of knowledge of the outcomes that were achieved last month, will be achieved this month, and have to be achieved in the next three months by those who report to you.

Question 6: As managers, we often talk about the need to align the work that our people do with the priorities we have set as managers.

While employees may know your priorities, rate their knowledge of what you do every day in your job — that is, what you didn't finish yesterday, what you are doing today, and what you have to do tomorrow.

Question 7: Rate your capacity to handle "things that have unexpectedly popped up" as well as "the unknown" — that you have to deal with?

And Watch It Happen Every Day!

PART III — YOUR PEOPLE

The challenge in work is that we have assumed that being hierarchical — that is, someone is in charge and others execute — will lead to a high level of success.

We know, however, that this model doesn't work.

The following questions get at important issues regarding those who work with and for you. Answer four of the following eight questions.

As the reality is you can't possibly know as much as those who are doing the work, you have to not just recognize their knowledge but also leverage that knowledge and their insights.

"I'll Teach You My Job!"

Question 1: Write a paragraph or two (or more) regarding what you see as the biggest strength — and the source of that strength — that those who work with and for you bring to the workplace.

And Watch It Happen Every Day!

Question 2: As a manager, supervisor, or an executive — anyone who is "in charge," in order to guide and focus the work of your people...

which of the following, if any, do you regard as the most essential task for you to put in place to improve the productivity of your people? Explain your choice(s).

- To set goals and develop and put in place a strategic plan.

- To hold periodic discussions with each of your employees.

- To measure performance against metrics.

- To develop work-related competencies and factors in professional development.

"I'll Teach You My Job!"

Question 3: On the weekend, you (a manager) do volunteer work as a lead carpenter and drywaller to construct new homes for the homeless. Also, your receptionist along with some neighbors and friends spend six hours each week after work and during the weekend as youth soccer coaches and officials.

What capacities do you and those who work with and for you share in these activities outside of work?

And Watch It Happen Every Day!

Question 4: Write a paragraph describing how you go about creating a commitment on your part to those who work with and for you.

"I'll Teach You My Job!"

Question 5: Write a paragraph or two as to whether commitment is the same as employment.

And Watch It Happen Every Day!

Question 6: There is a single paradigm shift that would get your and your people on the same page. What would that shift be?

"I'll Teach You My Job!"

Question 7: If I were to say that the single best change that would improve your management effectiveness is to eliminate "the role of the critic," what would you have to do that is different from long-standing management practices?

And Watch It Happen Every Day!

Question 8: If our work group falls short of achieving goals or finishing tasks or producing products correctly, as the manager, what would you say is the primary reason for the failure?

PART IV — BRINGING IT ALL TOGETHER: THE IMPACT OF THE TWICE-WEEKLY MEETINGS AND MAKING THOSE MEETINGS EFFECTIVE

Answer two of the five following questions:

Question 1: If you, as a manager, were to adopt the twice-weekly meetings — or even meet more frequently — write a paragraph or two regarding the changes you would have to make.

And Watch It Happen Every Day!

Question 2: Which of the major traditional management responsibilities would be assumed by the "employee-as-leader" who will run the twice-weekly meetings?

"I'll Teach You My Job!"

Question 3: As a manager, describe what you would see as the biggest benefit of the twice-weekly meetings.

And Watch It Happen Every Day!

Question 4: What would you see as other benefits from holding twice-weekly meetings?

"I'll Teach You My Job!"

Question 5: What would you say is the biggest reason that the twice-weekly meetings would be successful?

And Watch It Happen Every Day!

Book 10 — Are We Done Yet? No, We're Just Beginning... The Concrete Deliverables for Building Extraordinary Organizational Capacity

Part I: ISSUES FACING MANAGERS, SUPERVISORS, AND EXECUTIVES

If you're a manager, a supervisor, or an executive, **how would you** answer the following questions?

- What is your succession plan?
- What activities have you done this week to engage your employees?

- How are you assuring that the knowledge of your experienced individuals is captured and passed

"I'll Teach You My Job!"

on?

- What are you doing to retain your best people?
- What are you doing so that your people are getting the training they need to do their jobs superbly?

- How are you preparing your people for promotion and increased responsibility?
- What are you doing to enhance the employee experience?

If you're like most of us... if you're like me, even though you know these are all important, you would say something like,

"I think about it, **I know I should be** doing something, but I can't do it. I'm just too busy!"

And **those last words** are the key.

And Watch It Happen Every Day!

Because those of us who are managers and supervisors and executives are so busy doing our daily work and also trying to take care of whatever pops up,

we really have no time... **and can do very little** with these problems.

And because we also know that **we lack the knowledge and expertise** to effectively initiate, manage, and sustain projects like these,

what happens is our organizations step in —

because these problems that are found across offices and work groups aren't being addressed,

and **create special organization/business-wide programs** to take on and resolve each of these problems.

"I'll Teach You My Job!"

This Final Book is in Three Parts:

The first part is about the issues that all managers, supervisors, and executives know we should be doing something about if we and those who work with and for us are to be more productive and effective.

The second part focuses on why our typical organizational efforts to address these issues fall short. Whether we want to admit it, what we've done consistently for years is to rely on solutions even though **we know they don't work.**

The third part asks the important question: Because the problems still remain and must be solved, what can be done?

This final part **brings it all together...**

We go back to what we know. How we can we take on these issues through our daily work and how teaching my job – particularly HOW I/YOU manage — resolves these problems.

And Watch It Happen Every Day!

Programs such as:

- If we're having problems with finding people to move up into managerial or executive-level jobs,

  our organization/business creates a **succession program.**

- If we feel that our employees are not as enthusiastic as we'd like them to be about their work and/or our organizations,

  our organization/business creates an **employee engagement program.**

- If we're losing mission-critical people, we create a special **talent management program,**

"I'll Teach You My Job!"

a fast-track, intensive mentoring program with unique opportunities or assignments to develop certain individuals as future leaders.

- If we want to help our employees advance their careers, we create a **professional development program,**

  a curriculum with a number of courses that would "prepare" individuals to take on a new/higher level positions.

- And if organizations or businesses think that "The Employee Experience" is the key to success, we develop an "Employee Experience" initiative.

But even though our organizations put these programs in place, what we also know,

based on our experience with these programs, is that instead of being the "solutions" they are touted to be... for the most part, they fall short and aren't successful.

And since these problems are not getting solved by these programs that were designed to solve them,

don't we **have to conclude** that "these programs are not the right response to the problems."

Repeat: "These programs are not the right response to the problems."

Part II: WHY SPECIAL PROGRAMS IN OUR ORGANIZATIONS AND BUSINESS FALL SHORT AND FAIL

If we, the managers, supervisors, and executives, who are supposed to lead and manage our organizations or businesses, know that they're not the right response,

"I'll Teach You My Job!"

don't we have to ask ourselves **the obvious question**...

what is **the right response?** What should be done?

As a manager, I don't want to be told that I need to go to a particular program because we, as a company or an organization, have a problem. I value my time and will go to a program if doing so solves the problem(s) that I have; that makes me and my group more effective in our daily work. This isn't hard... solve my problem; that's what counts!

And Watch It Happen Every Day!

While there have been thousands of upbeat articles and hundreds of books written about these programs...

and that many of us have also read why these programs don't work and what should be done,

I found that **rather than providing** clarity and direction as to what I as a manager was supposed to do,

I instead found myself surrounded by this **"overwhelming fog"** of so many ideas and so much advice... that I couldn't decipher to find/get what I needed.

And **then, one day...**

"I'll Teach You My Job!"

like nearly everything else I had experienced as a manager where I and my colleagues **had figured out how to come to grips** with what we were facing...

what we had to and how to do it as part of our daily work,

BAM! That lightning bolt struck!

In our group, I and those who worked with and for me... **we didn't have** these problems!

As outrageous as it sounds to say that, it was true!

To start, nearly all organizations and businesses simply have stopped/given up on the biggest challenge — one that is **so large** that most organizations have given up trying to do something to deal with it...

And Watch It Happen Every Day!

And what is that challenge? The challenge is **knowledge transfer.**

Knowledge Transfer? Really??

We know this this is so important, but why this is such a challenge is that...

> whether you're the chief engineer, or a lead in product development, a fabricator, a machine tool operator, or an expert on supply chain management and procurement...

is that only you really have that knowledge that makes you effective...

"I'll Teach You My Job!"

the knowledge that enables you to do a job better than anyone else and come up with a superior product or the right answer.

And even though we all know your knowledge and skills are valuable — what we also know is that **businesses and organizations simply don't know** how to pass on your knowledge and skill.

As I've mentioned previously,

we have tried mentoring and coaching and high-level succession programs to prepare people to be ready to take on the work being done by someone else who is an acknowledged superior professional/performer...

>the work of a CEO, the work of a lead scientist, the work of a master carpenter, or that of a civil engineer.

And Watch It Happen Every Day!

But we have seen is that those programs fail to pass on the knowledge these individuals possess.

And the reason we know that they don't work — **is because what you did well** as that engineer or programmer or supply chain professional, as a manager or as an executive...

isn't done so well by those who replaced you because they make mistakes which leads to delays and costly rework and even failure.

In our group, we had not intended to take on and solve the knowledge transfer problem...

But, in the course of those twice-weekly meetings part of which was to talk about what each of us was working on, **we "shared"** also what we knew as to how best to do our jobs...

And **if knowledge transfer** means passing on the knowledge that each of us had... how best to do our jobs,

through those meetings which were part of our daily work, **we were doing exactly that!**

Part III: WHAT CAN BE DONE?

That I never faced the problem of the "loss of a person with critical knowledge" illustrates the impact of how we worked.

And Watch It Happen Every Day!

When I first came on board, it was clear that I had inherited a "very dysfunctional office." I don't think I can ever fully convey **how much people had hated** this office.

I met people who simply had to express their anger about things that had happened/not happened over a decade earlier! They hadn't forgotten…

They hated this office because it had failed nearly every time to do what we had been asked to provide or simply had done it wrong!

When I came on board, I got rid of some staff and relocated others…

And in one year, I replaced the entire staff — some of whom were egregiously bad!

"I'll Teach You My Job!"

I hired new people...

----

*I had a dysfunctional person who was the benefits officer who **consistently overpromised** and seldom delivered... who didn't enroll people.*

We did no training for employees and there was no professional development for managers and supervisors.

*And it was beyond anyone's imagination to think that **somehow we could train leadership...***

*We were terrible at employment. Job ads would take weeks to get done and then it would take months to set up interviews and inform offices as to who was still available to hire. Of course, **all of this delay** meant the best people had gotten other jobs and were no longer available.*

I replaced the benefits person and in the course of the

And Watch It Happen Every Day!

next 12 months, I turned over the entire staff of the office.

*Some had wanted to leave – they **were burnt out** by all the constant barrage of criticism and others knew their interests were elsewhere...*

*I did everything I could to move people to better jobs. They were not at fault; they were **simply shell-shocked** by what they had to endure every day!*

*But even with a new employment person and a new head of benefits, it was clear that we **didn't have enough.***

----

and they joined the others in the group...

And through the twice-weekly meetings, they quickly picked up on who was doing what, **specifically** what needed to be done.

"I'll Teach You My Job!"

So, when the senior professional left... a development which **would cripple** many operations for some time,

that simply didn't happen!

The two others plus an individual who had been transferred to us from another group... because **they knew** what was going on through the twice-weekly meetings,

simply picked up the workload.

And **instead of spending four months** to two years... finding a new person and getting that individual up to speed,

we had the people on board who **just stepped in** and did the work... and didn't miss a beat!

And Watch It Happen Every Day!

And later, when each of those people moved to other organizations — they had become so good others wanted to hire them...

we still **didn't miss a beat...** because others in the group also knew their jobs and were able to step up and step in and get the job done.

So, the loss of a "critical person" **never adversely impacted us.**

And it readily follows that I never tried to import someone else's succession program... I always had someone in place ready to do what was needed.

I didn't even think of setting up a special mentoring program with special assignments or projects because people knew the work that had to be done.

"I'll Teach You My Job!"

and the thought of a special talent development program **simply never crossed my mind** because, as they learned the work of others, they were becoming "highly desirable" colleagues.

I never set up a professional development program or a performance plan with goals and objectives…

I never had to do a performance improvement plan or had difficulty doing anyone's performance evaluation… because we knew on a daily basis what was being done and what needed further attention.

And I never sent anyone to a management development program or a supervisor training course either.

Why not? All of these just happened as **part of our daily work.**

And Watch It Happen Every Day!

___

I remember going to conferences and meetings... and listening to presenters talking about these special programs,

or reading articles and books related to the challenges I listed at the beginning of this book,

and I realized that **we didn't have** these problems...

And we didn't have these problems was because of HOW we had worked together — **particularly through the twice-weekly meetings.**

"I'll Teach You My Job!"

Thus, whether it was succession, knowledge transfer,

or employee engagement, professional development, talent development,

management development or supervisor training, or leadership training,

or preparing people for greater responsibility or promotion, and thereby retaining our people,

or having a workplace where the employee experience was positive and fulfilling,

we didn't have these problems and challenges....

And Watch It Happen Every Day!

because all of these were simply outcomes of HOW we did our daily work and how we managed!

So, rather than being the problems described at the beginning of this Book 10...

> problems that are pretty much unresolved and unaddressed in large part in offices and workgroups across an organization or a business,

because they are outcomes of our daily work and how we managed...

they really are "concrete deliverables" of organization-wide impact that any

"I'll Teach You My Job!"

manager, supervisor, or executive can deliver!

I entitled this book, "I'll Teach You My Job"... and the various books described what we did and how we did it.

I strongly encourage you to read the entire book again... and write down your observations, thoughts, and possible actions in the book or the pages for notes at the end of each book or in a notebook if you are ready the e-book version.

I think you'll find it valuable.

And doing so will not only make this book your own, you may well be taking the steps to put you on the path to make you superbly effective!

And Watch It Happen Every Day!

THE CLOSING NOTE:

We did this with no approval from the individual I reported to.

We did this with no checklist or template.

We did this without reference to a model or "best practices."

And it's the same for you...

whether you're a manager, an employee, a supervisor, a team leader, a director, a division head, or an executive,

"I'll Teach You My Job!"

---

you can have impact by what you do in your office, your workgroup and/or team or on an organization-wide basis,

Just remember, it doesn't need to be a special program. It can happen just as part of daily work...

because of HOW we, that is, each of us — who is a manager, an employee, a supervisor, a director, a division head, or an executive...

chooses to lead and manage and how we work with those who work with and for us.

Is the light bulb flickering?

BAM!

The Appendix

How to Read This Book

This is a narrative –a story about **my "struggles" as a manager** – not just the first time I was in the role, but at various times throughout my career.

Just because I've held different jobs at different levels with increasing responsibility over the years doesn't mean I suddenly became flawless.

Every job was something new and different, so I had to come up with ways to address the challenges to be able to manage a robust, successful operation.

And just like I had to innovate to be effective in my jobs, I realized that if this book is to be meaningful to you, the reader,

"I'll Teach You My Job!"

I had to lay out/format this book in **an innovative way that would connect with you!**

Thus, the language, the way I say things, the expressions I use — are the way I talk at work. It's colloquial and relational, not textbook English.

You'll also different formatting – designed to be "Easy to Read and Quick to Learn!"

So, why did I do this?

I wrote this as a narrative because...

Amy, just a fabulous friend who in listening to me talk about what I was trying to write, said, **"Ken, you're telling a story!"**

And she was right! Amy gave me the perfect "on-target" insight —

And Watch It Happen Every Day!

and when I started writing to tell a story — **it became very clear real quick** that it was the best style to convey what I went through.

So, by telling a story that I think you can relate to,

the narrative gave me the best way **to express —**

the struggles, and the amazing insights and realizations, followed by what felt like **magical breakthroughs** where suddenly things just fell into place!

that I went through!

Thus, whether you're the CEO or a manager, a supervisor, or a division head, **being able to**

"I'll Teach You My Job!"

manage well is a serious responsibility.

In our jobs, regardless of the title of our position, we all bear that heavy burden…

that "being charge" — having high-profile, "the buck stops here" responsibilities…

is far from easy.

And it doesn't matter whatever level we work…

things you/I don't know well enough or aren't open to hearing or learning **can inflict serious damage on you/us** as well as those who work with and for you/me, and also our businesses or organizations.

So, back to how this book is written… specifically the layout and grammar.

As you read this book – what you'll notice immediately is that **there are only six or so sentences per**

And Watch It Happen Every Day!

page…

with **words written in larger font size** - like 20 for most words and **26 bolded** for other words or phrases.

And there are **double line spaces** often and sometimes even a larger number of line spaces used.

When there are more line spaces than two, I did this because I wanted **to create a way to transition** from a group of sentences that worked together,

and the three or four line spaces are a way to signal that we would be moving on to a new thought, idea, or point.

There were other reasons why I also wrote the narrative this way.

"I'll Teach You My Job!"

I don't know about you, but for me, there is just too much "word-clutter" in most books!

I know that trying to read **"text-dense books"** with multi-sentence paragraphs crammed together...

made it difficult to remember what I had read...

and when I went back to search for a particular piece of information — a thought, a phrase — I found that difficult to do as well.

So, because of these experiences, I decided to write a book in a style that would overcome these obstacles...

The result:

And Watch It Happen Every Day!

A book **written in an "Easy to Read" and "Quick to Learn!" layout**...

where, instead of being "text-dense"...

there are six or so sentences per page,

variable font sizes and the use of bolding for some words — sometimes a few words,

but on other occasions a complete sentence or a number of consecutive sentences.

There is also **unique spacing to create a sense** that a group sentences fit together... and to also **to indicate a transition** to a new thought.

And to further the ease of reading the book, I took some liberties with grammar and punctuation...

"I'll Teach You My Job!"

that your English teacher would seriously object to!

You'll see things like (not, such as):

- **Prepositions at the end** of sentences: "These are the things we need to take care of."

- You'll see split infinitives…

- And what seems like Illogical ellipses… why is he using those?

- **You'll also see things like s/he** (rather than she and he), his/her as well as I/you or you/us…

    I know this is not so unusual, but I did this because writing "he or she" and so forth just drew out a sentence unnecessarily without adding much.

And Watch It Happen Every Day!

I also want to bring to your attention that **when I write something like "I/you"...**

the intent is to have you understand that, while what I'm writing about is about me,

I wanted you, the reader, to know that I think it's just as important that the writing may also be meaningful and possibly applicable to and connects with you.

So, yes, I could have written "we" but **I didn't want to presume that you** would agree because I really don't if in fact you would...

and thus you have the choice of accepting/not accepting what I've written as meaningful/applicable to you.

Other reasons why I wrote this way

This book is a narrative, which means I try write the way people talk or may be thinking.

"I'll Teach You My Job!"

When we talk, very few of us remember to eliminate dangling prepositions or that we should avoid putting an adverb between the infinitive.

When people talk, they **use adverbs for emphasis** — "... to really reach out and talk with our clients."

They don't say, "It's important to remember to reach out and talk with our clients." (Well, some of us do/might, but, again, it isn't how most people talk at work.)

And when I had written earlier drafts of the book following professional grammar rules —

> like what you'd find in an essay, a magazine article, a report, or books,

I just found it so difficult to say things enthusiastically!

And, if you're a manager or a leader, there's one thing

And Watch It Happen Every Day!

we know, you have to inspire and motivate if you want things to happen! So, whenever I have to choose between form and enthusiasm, **I opted for enthusiasm!**

A few more comments:

While writing this narrative, I also found that certain grammar conventions got in the way of the message.

For example, **I use a lot of ellipses** in this book.

When I was advised that I had to use the standard ellipse convention, I found that doing so added nothing. In fact, it made sentences longer and drag on unnecessarily.

My thinking behind using the ellipses was different.

I wanted to use the ellipse to connect thoughts...

"I'll Teach You My Job!"

to convey a sense that I was trying to think this through... **that I was pondering...**

which then led to a realization, a new insight, a different perspective or an approach that worked!

And here's an important comment:

You will also see a number of different word combinations like...

> **"higher level responsibility/more complex work"**
>
> **"to bring about/further their own success"**
>
> **"the decline/failure"**

And Watch It Happen Every Day!

I know that connecting these words by the **"/"** is hardly ever done.

But I combined them because I wanted to convey that what we're doing is not just describable by one word or verb...

that, because we are not all the same, as we're distinct individuals, each of may not be in just one state or circumstance but possibly/likely two if not more.

I also had another reason for combining the words through the use of the slash — **"the word/word combination."** I did this because I wanted to convey that, at some point, even though they represent different states of being at a particular point in time or actions that might be or are being taken...

the words being connected by the **"/"** are related... and that you, the reader, should consider the implications of both.

"I'll Teach You My Job!"

Finally, you'll see that I'm kind of "old school" in part.

I do use two spaces after the period to end a sentence. I know the convention now is that a single space is now pretty much the norm.

But the double space is still acceptable, and the reason I use the double space is again "readability."

And what I said about the "two space" leads to a final comment which ties back to how I use the ellipse.

If we can change from double space after a period, why can't we get rid of the (space) . (space) . (space) . and simply use … when adding/using an ellipse in a sentence?

As I said, my goal is content and substance.

When form or style helps, I'll use it, but, as I said, I'm more interested in connecting with you —

If this book and its ideas and how it's written make

And Watch It Happen Every Day!

sense to you, and you put some or all of the ideas in place, maybe they can help you **become a better manager/leader...**

And because you're a better manager, you may well find that what you want to accomplish will happen, and, best of all,

because they will be meaningful to those who work with and for you,

"All of you will be in sync... working together so that there is nothing you can't take on!"

Enjoy reading "I'll Teach You My Job!"

"I'll Teach You My Job!"

Page for Notes

And Watch It Happen Every Day!

Page for Notes

"I'll Teach You My Job!"

Page for Notes